# CONTENTS

# 1. First Things First

So you are interested in baseball. Would you like some tips on how to play a better game? Do you want to find out about some of the fine points that professional players and umpires know?

This book will explain the rules, terms, and theory of the game, and will offer tips to help you become a better ballplayer.

### Two-Player Baseball

Baseball can be played on vacant lots, in fields, pastures, or in fine ball parks built especially for the purpose. No matter where the game is played, four things are needed — a ball, a bat, players, and an area large enough to play on.

The simplest form of baseball is a game between two players. One player has the ball and the other the bat. For a two-player game any ball may be used, and any piece of wood may serve as bat.

The player with the ball, the *pitcher*, stands at a certain distance from a spot called home base.

The player with the bat, the *batter*, stands beside home base. He will stand at the right or left of the base according to whether he bats right-handed or left-handed.

In a two-player game, or a sand-lot game, playing space is not marked out. In a regular game, the batter must stand within a *batter's box*. This box is a rectangle four feet wide and six feet long, and the inside line is six inches from home base. The batter's box contains as much area in front of the base as behind the base; the batter may stand anywhere inside the batter's box but he cannot step outside the boundary lines of the batter's box.

In a two-player game, or sand-lot games, any flat object may be used for home base. The official *Baseball Rules** say that home base in a real game shall be a five-sided slab of whitened rubber seventeen inches wide and must measure seventeen inches from the side facing the pitcher to the point facing the catcher.

Ballplayers usually call the home base *home plate*.

---

* The book of official *Baseball Rules* is published by The National Baseball Congress of America. Copies may usually be obtained at any sporting goods store and always by writing The National Baseball Congress of America, Wichita, Kansas.

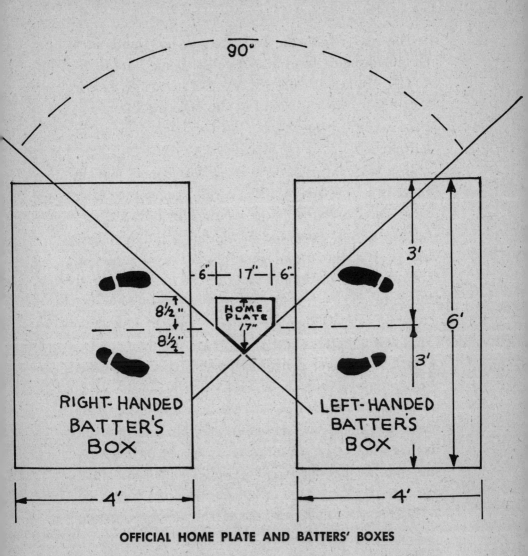

90"

6" | 17" | 6"

HOME
PLATE
17"

8½"
8½"

3'

6'

3'

RIGHT-HANDED
BATTER'S
BOX

LEFT-HANDED
BATTER'S
BOX

4'

4'

**OFFICIAL HOME PLATE AND BATTERS' BOXES**

## STRIKE ZONE

Sometimes they just call it "the plate." The size and shape of the plate and batters' boxes are shown in the diagram on page 7 as they are given in the official *Baseball Rules*.

The pitcher tries to throw the ball so that the batter cannot make a hit. He must pitch the ball into the *strike zone,* that is, the space above home plate extending from the batter's armpits to the top of his knees when he is standing in his usual batter's position. If the batter does not swing at the pitch, and the umpire decides that the ball was in the strike zone, he will call the pitch a *strike*. It is also a strike if the batter swings at the ball and misses it, even if the pitch was not in the strike zone.

8

If the batter hits the ball foul, it is a strike too, except that a foul ball does not count as a strike after the batter has two strikes against him. In other words, a foul ball never counts as the third strike, except when the foul comes from a deliberate attempt to *bunt* (jab at the ball with a loosely-held bat) after two strikes and the ball rolls foul. There are several other types of foul balls. Bunting and foul balls are explained later in the book (see Index for page numbers).

A batter is permitted three strikes. He is *out* after three strikes, whether he swings at the ball and fails to hit it, or does not swing at a ball that the umpire rules was in the strike zone.

When a pitch is not in the strike zone and the batter does not swing at it, it is called a *ball*. Four balls pitched to a batter give him a *base on balls*. He is allowed to go to first base with no risk of being put out. In a two-player, or in a sand-lot, game the batter is not allowed to walk but must hit the ball in order to go to first base. In a regular game, any runners on base when the batter receives a base on balls also move up a base without risk of being put out. Making a *put-out*, or being put out, is more fully discussed on page 12.

The batter tries to hit the ball far enough so that he can run to one or more bases without being put out. In a simple two-player game, however, there is

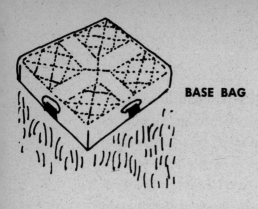

BASE BAG

only one base beside home plate. A put-out is made if the pitcher can get the batted ball back to the plate before the batter can run to the other base and return to home base. Sometimes the two players change places after every put-out. Sometimes they play without changing until two or three put-outs are made.

This two-player game, frequently played in cities, is sometimes called *one o'cat, one eye cat,* or *one old cat.*

### Work-up Baseball

Suppose more players join the game. There may be enough so that there are two or three batters. In this case, there will be two or three bases besides home base.

In a regular game, the rules say there shall be a first base, a second base, and a third base. They also say that these bases shall be white canvas bags that are fifteen inches square, and no less than three inches or more than five inches thick. They shall be filled with soft material and securely fastened to the ground.

The diagrams of the layout of a baseball field shown in Chapter 2 indicate where the bases should be located. But in less than nine-player games, bases may be less than official.

With two or three batters and several players to catch, stop, or chase batted balls – but not enough players to choose sides – the game is called *work-up*, because each player works up to bat. One player, the catcher, stands behind the batter, behind home plate, and he catches pitches that are not hit.

When a batter makes an out in work-up, the catcher moves up to the batter's position. The pitcher moves to the catcher's position. Another player moves to the pitcher's place, and every other player moves one step nearer to becoming the batter. Each player tries to get the batter out so that he can work up to a turn at bat.

### Scrub Baseball

When there are enough players to form sides, the game becomes *scrub*. In a scrub game, there may be more or fewer than nine players to a side. One side plays the field. Its team includes a pitcher, catcher, basemen, and fielders. The other side is at bat until three of its men make outs. Then the sides change: the team that was in the field comes up to bat; the side that has batted goes into the field.

There are different ways that put-outs are made. A batter becomes a put-out when he strikes out; when he hits a fly ball that is caught by a fielder before it touches the ground or anything fastened to the ground; when a fielder grabs a ball which has hit the ground and gets it to the base before the batter reaches that base.

A baserunner becomes an out when he is *tagged* (touched) with the ball when he is not on a base;

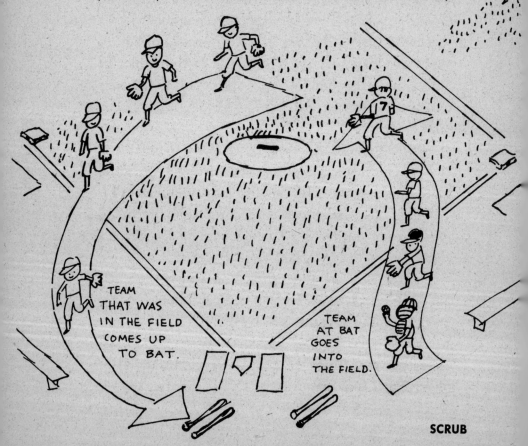

TEAM THAT WAS IN THE FIELD COMES UP TO BAT.

TEAM AT BAT GOES INTO THE FIELD.

SCRUB

when he is trying to reach a base in advance of the base he was on and the ball is held by a fielder on that base before he reaches it. This is known as a *force out*, because the runner was forced to leave the base he was on when a player following him became entitled to that base.

A player cannot be forced when a batter following him receives a base on balls. Every runner ahead of the man earning a base on balls is legally entitled to the base ahead of him, and cannot be put out.

A batter may hit a *single*, a hit that allows him to go to first base. If a player in the field fumbles or misses the ball, so that he cannot throw it to the base in time, the batter is safe on first base by the fielder's *error*.

A batter may hit the ball far enough or hit it to a spot a fielder cannot reach in time, and get to second base. This is a *two-base hit*. Players sometimes call it a *double*. If a ball is batted far enough, the batter might reach third base. This is a *three-base hit* or a *triple*.

Suppose you are the batter, and you hit the ball out of the park, or so far you can run around all the bases without being put out. You have hit a *home run!* A homer! You are a long-ball hitter! A slugger! Team-mates will rush to shake your hand as you cross the plate. For a few minutes you feel like Babe Ruth or

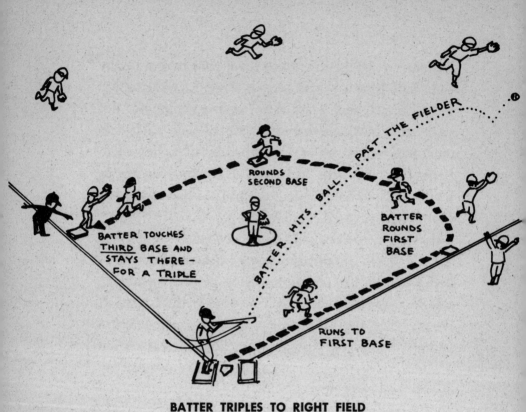

**BATTER TRIPLES TO RIGHT FIELD**

Roger Maris or Willie Mays or Hank Aaron or another famous home-run slugger!

### Regulation Game

As you know, every regulation game has certain features that never change. According to official baseball rules a game is played between two teams of nine players each. Each player goes to the plate to bat when it is his turn. Each team tries to score more runs than the other. The game is set up for nine innings during which each team is at bat in each inning. But no matter how many innings are played, each side must have the same number of chances to be at bat. If anything happens to keep a team from having its final chance to bat, the score returns to that of the last complete inning.

A *run* is made when a team succeeds in getting one of its players around the bases without that player being put out. An *inning* has been played when each side has been at bat until it has made three outs. If the score is tied at the end of nine innings, extra innings are played. The game goes on until one team has more runs than the other and both have had an equal number of turns at bat.

### Games Not Always Nine Innings

The official *Baseball Rules* provide only for nine-inning games, unless shortened by weather conditions. Frequently high-school games, some second games of double-headers, and games played by teams younger than high-school age are played as seven-inning games, or less. Leagues of young players often limit the competition to six innings. This does not mean that a shorter-than-nine-inning game is less than real baseball.

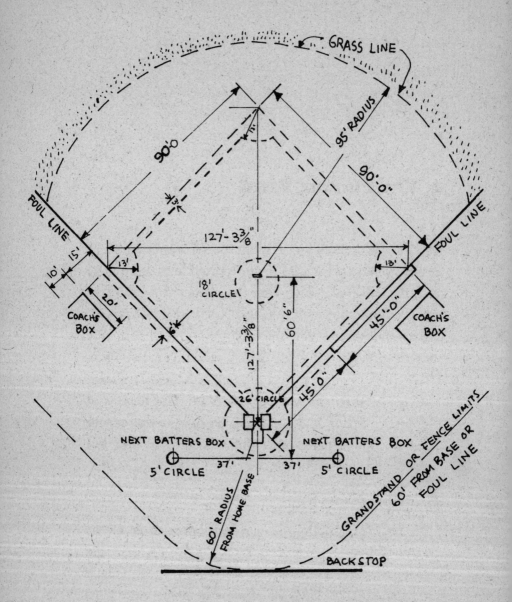

GRASS LINE

90'0"

95' RADIUS

90'-0"

FOUL LINE

FOUL LINE

127'-3⅜"

18' CIRCLE

60'-6"

127'-3⅜"

45'-0"

10'

15'

13'

13'

COACH'S BOX

20'

COACH'S BOX

45'-0"

26' CIRCLE

NEXT BATTERS BOX

NEXT BATTERS BOX

5' CIRCLE

37'

37'

5' CIRCLE

GRANDSTAND OR FENCE LIMITS
60' FROM BASE OR FOUL LINE

60' RADIUS FROM HOME BASE

BACKSTOP

**DIAMOND OR INFIELD**

## 2. The Playing Field

HIGH SCHOOLS, colleges, recreational leagues, and all professionally organized leagues provide playing areas just for baseball. They are based on an infield of standard measurements which is called a *diamond*.

The diamond, or infield, is really a ninety-foot square that spreads out from one corner which is home plate. Home plate is marked by a plate of hard white rubber. Facing the diamond from home plate, first base is at the corner to the right, second base is at the corner opposite home plate, and third base is at the left corner, opposite first base.

### Pitcher's Plate and Mound

In your imagination draw a line between first base and third base. Half way along this line is a rectangle twenty-four inches long and six inches wide. This is the *pitcher's plate*. It is usually made of the same hard

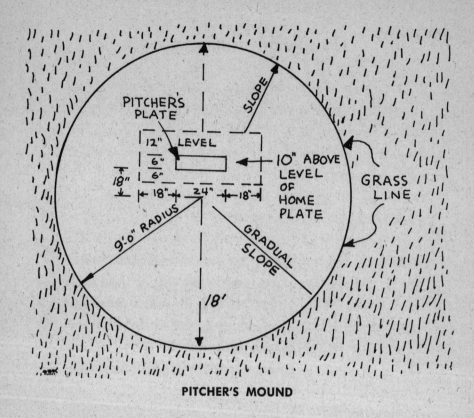

PITCHER'S MOUND

rubber as home plate. Sportswriters often call it *the rubber* or *the slab*.

The front edge of the pitcher's rectangle (rubber) must lie sixty feet and six inches from the back point of home plate. The rubber is ten inches higher than home plate. The ground around the rubber slopes gradually downward to home plate level and forms the *pitcher's mound*, which is eighteen feet in diameter. This is a sloping area.

**SIDE VIEW OF PITCHER'S MOUND**

It is little wonder that the pitcher's box is sometimes called the *mound* or *hill*. It is easy to understand why a pitcher who is hit hard enough to be removed from the game is said to be *knocked off the hill, shelled off the mound,* or *batted out of the box.*

### Foul Lines

Beginning at the back point of home plate, a line is drawn to first base and on outward, all the way to the right-field fence or to the beginning of the stands (if there are stands). The same kind of line runs from home plate to third base, and on outward to the left-field fence, or to the beginning of the stands. These are the *foul lines.* They are usually made with a line-marker filled with the kind of lime that does not burn flesh or grass.

From first base to second base, and from second base to third base there are no drawn lines, only imaginary lines. The marked foul lines from home plate to first base and from home plate to third, and the unmarked lines from first base to second and from second to third, form the diamond.

The part of the ballfield inside the diamond is the *infield.* The portion of the ballfield outside the diamond is the outfield.

19

### Fair and Foul Balls

A ball batted into the air beyond the infield must stay between the foul lines to be a fair ball. A ball batted onto the ground must stay between the foul lines going past first base or third base to be a fair ball.

Only fair balls permit the batter to become a baserunner. Usually men already on base can advance only on fair balls. An exception to this rule occurs when a foul ball batted into the air is caught. In this case, a baserunner may advance at his own risk. Either a foul ball or a fair ball hit into the air and caught before touching the ground causes the batter to be out.

The distance from home plate along the foul lines to the fence or stands is not always the same. It varies according to how much space there is.

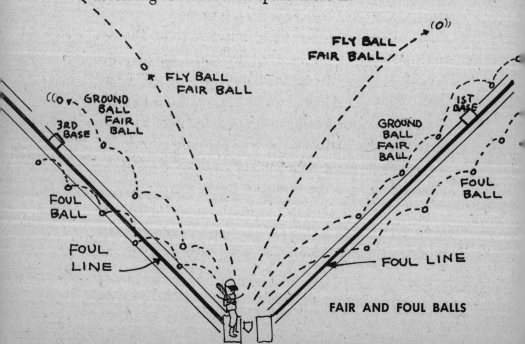

FAIR AND FOUL BALLS

Sometimes fences are too close to home plate. One way in which the problem is solved is to erect a tall screen which the ball must clear to give the batter a home run. A ball that hits the screen and stays in the ball park is in play, which means the batter takes his chance at being put out at any base he tries for. This is what the Los Angeles Dodgers did in Memorial Coliseum where they played until Dodger Stadium was completed.

Another way that the two teams solve the space problem is by agreeing to ground rules before playing. The ground rule may limit a batter who hits the ball over a low fence (one that is less than the normal distance from home plate) to two bases.

### Grass Lines

The diagram in the official *Baseball Rules* shows a grass line in two places. One marks the circular area of outfield grass beyond the bare – or "skinned" – base paths. This grass line is an arc drawn from foul line to foul line with a radius of ninety-five feet from the center of the pitcher's rubber. The other grass line forms a circle around the pitcher's mound at a distance of nine feet from the center of the rubber.

Professional-league ball parks and most college ball-fields have a grass infield with bare base paths and pitcher's mound. Plenty of other diamonds are laid

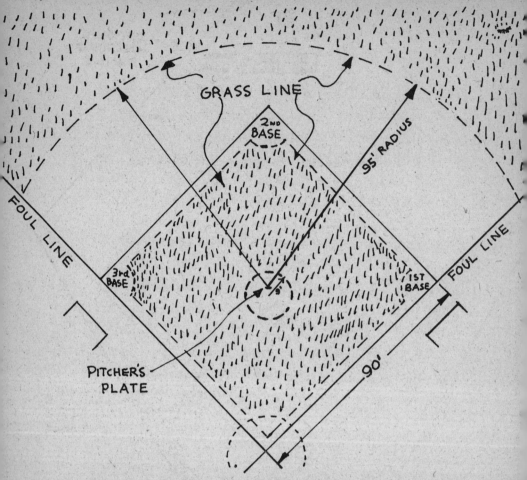

**DIAGRAM OF GRASS LINES (as shown in official *Baseball Rules*)**

out in areas where there is no grass. Nothing in the rules forbids this.

Most leagues for younger players feel that the regulation baseball field should be made smaller for younger players. Here is a diagram of the Little League baseball field for players under thirteen.

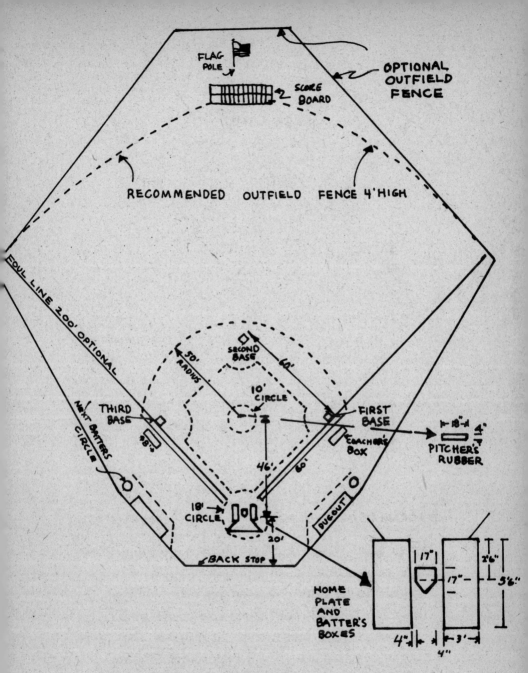

**LITTLE LEAGUE BALLFIELD (for players under thirteen)**

# 3. Equipment

## The Uniform

Official baseball rules specify that the uniforms of all players on a team must be exactly alike in color, trim, and style. Any part of an undershirt that is exposed must be of the same color for all players on that team. A player whose uniform differs from those of his teammates will not be allowed to play in a game.

The club insignia, the numbers, and the letters may be of a different color from the uniform itself. Aside from these, no material of another color may be fastened onto it. Nothing that imitates or suggests the shape of a baseball may be part of a uniform. No glass buttons or any shiny metal may be used. This rule was made because reflections from the sun, or lights in a night game, might flash in a batter's eyes! A player must not attach anything to his shoe other than the ordinary shoe plate or toe plate.

All games played under the rules of organized baseball try to enforce the rules for uniforms. However, beginners in Little League or other recreational leagues all over the country are not always expected to live up to every regulation.

In a sand-lot game, just as good baseball may be played in assorted uniforms, or no uniforms at all. It is recommended, though, that even sand-lot players wear protective helmets, especially while batting.

As for equipment other than uniforms, here is what the rules tell us.

### The Baseball

The official baseball is a core of cork, rubber, or similar material with yarn wound around it, covered on the outside with two pieces of white horsehide stitched tightly together. The ball must weigh between five and five-and-one-fourth ounces. It must not measure less than nine inches or more than nine-and-one-fourth inches around.

SIDE VIEW OF CUT-AWAY BASEBALL

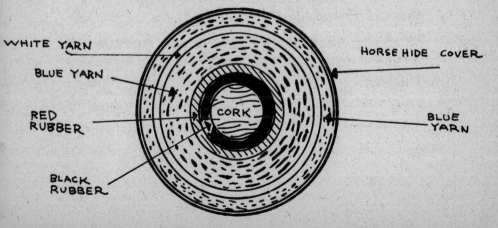

WHITE YARN

BLUE YARN

RED RUBBER

BLACK RUBBER

CORK

HORSE HIDE COVER

BLUE YARN

These dimensions hold for all hard-ball games, from Little League upward.

When you hold a baseball in your hand, you can feel the seam made by the slanted stitches which hold the pieces of leather together. The raised seam is a great help to a pitcher gripping the ball for a fast ball, curve, slider, sinker, change-up, or knuckler. These are pitches you will read more about in Chapter 9.

### The Bat

The official baseball bat must be made of wood. Pieces of wood bonded together may be used, or the bat may be one solid piece. But in every bat, the grain of all the wood must run parallel to the length of the bat. Most bats are made from one piece of solid and well-seasoned wood.

The bat must be smooth and round, with no flat surface area. At the thickest part it must not measure more than two-and-three-fourths inches in diameter. In length it must not be more than forty-two inches. The handle end of the bat may be roughened or wrapped with tape or twine for no more than eighteen inches from the bottom of the bat.

There is no rule regarding the weight of the bat.

For the beginning ballplayer the best bat is the one that suits him. Never settle on a bat simply because it is the model used by some famous big-league hitter. His size and needs are different from yours.

### Protective Clothing

When it comes to what the catcher of a team will wear, the rule book is generous. Here are the items he is allowed to wear: a leather glove or *mitt* of any size, shape, or weight; shin guards; mask; and chest protector.

A catcher can certainly use all these things. In his position behind the batter, he must catch balls pitched as fast as his pitcher can throw. Sometimes he must stop *foul tips* (balls merely tipped by the bat when it is swung), which come

**CATCHER'S EQUIPMENT**

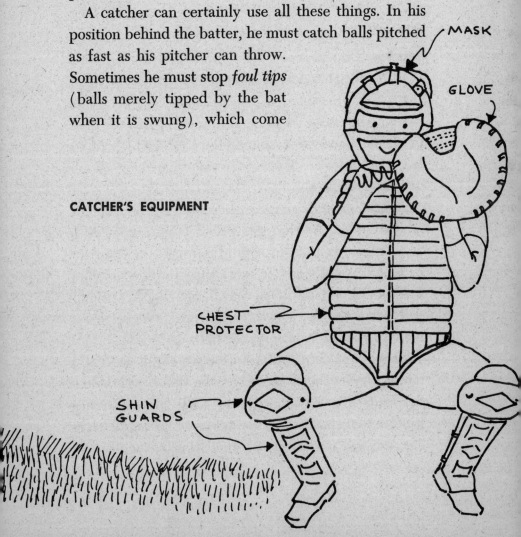

MASK

GLOVE

CHEST PROTECTOR

SHIN GUARDS

back very fast. Or suppose a player on the other team is trying to reach home plate. He often slides, feet forward, with the metal cleats on the bottoms of his shoes exposed. The catcher's job is to block him. This is another time when he really needs his special equipment.

### The Glove

The *first baseman* must catch balls thrown hard to him by other players. One of his most important jobs is to catch these throws and touch first base before the player who hit the ball gets there. The rules permit the first baseman to wear a leather glove or mitt not more than twelve inches long from top to bottom. It cannot be more than eight inches wide across the palm, from the base of the thumb crotch to the outer edge of the mitt.

At times some first basemen have tried to use mitts which were more like butterfly nets. This gave them an unfair advantage. For this reason there are restrictions now on the size, shape, web, and depth of pocket of a first baseman's mitt.

Each player in the field other than the first baseman and catcher may also wear a leather glove. It usually is different from the mitt-type glove in that it provides separate compartments for each finger and the thumb. It is limited in size to the same length and width as the first baseman's mitt. There is no weight limitation.

**FIRST BASEMAN'S GLOVE**      **FIELDER'S OR PITCHER'S GLOVE**

However, the webbing between thumb and fingers may not be of wound or wrapped lacing to form a net or trap-type mitt. Ballplayers sometimes refer to the fielder's glove as a *finger mitt*.

The pitcher's glove must be all one color, the rules tell us, but must not be white or gray. No foreign material may be fastened to it.

Baseball rules have been made and changed when necessary for good reasons. For example, in 1946 a United States Army timing device tested fast balls pitched by Bob Feller, one of baseball's great speed-ball pitchers. His fast ball was clocked at 146 feet per second at the pitching distance of sixty feet, six inches. This means the ball came at the batter at a speed of ninety-nine-and-a-half miles per hour! At that speed a batter just cannot have his vision distracted by anything! For this reason, it is important for the batter to wear a batting helmet.

### Sliding Pads and Shoes

Sliding pads to protect the hips are not required by the rules but most players wear them under their uniforms. They help prevent "strawberries" – the raw red spots left when skin is scraped off in making a slide.

You probably know the term *spikes* – the name ballplayers have given to their shoes because of the triangular metal plates or cleats on the soles. The shoes are made of soft lightweight leather, sometimes of kangaroo skin. Baseball can be played without spikes but these special shoes make it easier for a player to stop quickly, and they prevent slipping. A real ballplayer, of course, will use his spikes properly. It is never his purpose to come onto a base in such a way as to injure an opponent.

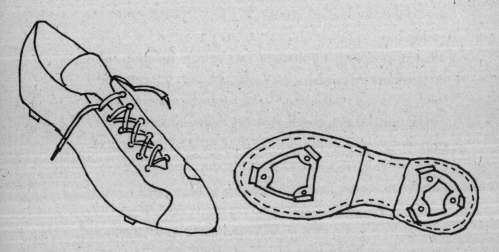

**BASEBALL SHOES WITH CLEATS**

# 4. A Made-up Inning

Now LET's SAY that we have a place to play, a baseball, and a bat. Or perhaps there will be several bats,
since each player needs one that fits him. We also have
a pitcher's rubber, a home plate, canvas bags for the
other three bases, and two teams of nine boys each.

First of all, everybody should take part in a warm-
ing-up session. It is foolish for any player – even a
young boy – to throw hard until he has loosened up his
muscles properly. Otherwise, he can ruin his arm. Big-
league stars invariably give young players the same advice: treasure your arm. Never try to throw very hard
or fast while you are still growing. Muscles that are not
fully developed should not be subjected to the strain of
overthrowing. Besides, you may acquire poor throwing
habits.

While the players are warming up for our imaginary
inning, let's talk about *line-up* and *batting order*. A little has already been said about the pitcher, catcher,

and first baseman. Later on there will be more about what individual players do at each of the nine positions on a team. For the time being, we need to know only about the following things.

Just as the *first baseman* takes throws made to first base, so the *second baseman* takes throws to second base, and the *third baseman* takes throws to third.

The *shortstop* protects the area *between* second and third base. He also takes throws made *to* second base when the second baseman is not near enough to cover it himself.

The first baseman, second baseman, third baseman, and shortstop are the *infielders*. Their job is to keep balls batted into their territory from becoming *base hits*. A base hit occurs when a batted ball is fair, no error is made, and a batter reaches base safely.

An infielder tries to catch any ball batted in the air (fly ball or foul) that he can reach. He fields a ball batted into his territory by catching, stopping, or scooping it up in his glove. Although they always try, infielders often cannot reach the ball in time.

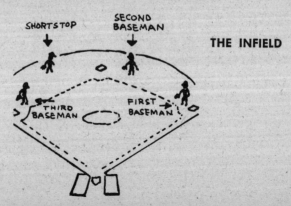

SHORTSTOP  SECOND BASEMAN

THE INFIELD

THIRD BASEMAN  FIRST BASEMAN

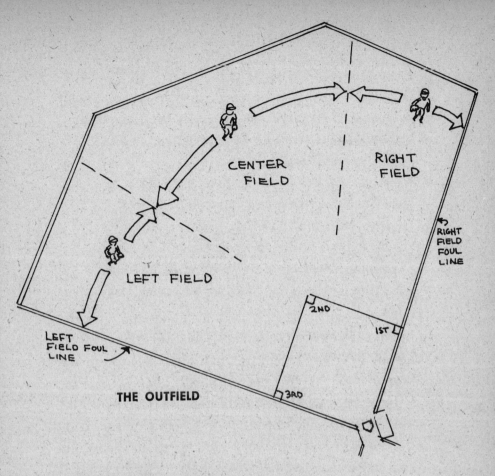

CENTER FIELD

RIGHT FIELD

RIGHT FIELD FOUL LINE

LEFT FIELD

2ND

1ST

LEFT FIELD FOUL LINE

THE OUTFIELD

3RD

The outfield is made up of three parts: left field, center field, and right field. The parts are named in relation to a view from home plate, not from the fielder's view. The *left fielder* covers left field, of course. It is his job to field balls batted on the ground (*grounders*) when they get past the third baseman and shortstop. He is also expected to catch any fly ball he can reach when it is batted into his territory. This includes about one third of the outfield, from the left-field foul line toward center, as well as any area he can get to *outside* the left-field foul line.

The *center fielder* patrols the center third of the outfield. He must catch balls batted into the air in this area. It is also his duty to field grounders that are hit past the shortstop and second baseman into his territory.

Right field is the third of the outfield from center field to the right-field foul line. A *right fielder* tries to catch the ball in the air if it is a fly, either in fair ground or foul territory outside the right-field foul line. He also fields grounders that get past the first baseman and second baseman, into his territory.

No matter what position a player may have in the field, when his team is at bat he has a definite place in the *batting order*. This is decided before the game and cannot be changed. Whether or not a player is taken from the game, or moved to another position, his place in the batting order remains the same. Any substitute for him must bat in that same place. You can easily see how unfair it would be for teams to move their best batters around and send them to the plate whenever they choose.

All right, everybody has warmed up. Let's see about starting the game.

We have someone to be the umpire. He will decide whether pitches are in the strike zone and are strikes, or are outside the strike zone and are balls. He will say when men are safe on plays at the bases and when they are out. And he will decide whether a batted ball is fair or foul. A baseball game can be played without an umpire. But it goes much more smoothly when an umpire, rather than the players, makes the decisions.

"Play ball!" the umpire calls. "Batter up!"

The *lead-off man* (first player) in the batting order of the team at bat takes his place at the plate. The pitcher is ready. He delivers the first pitch of the game. It is in the strike zone but our batter doesn't swing at it.

"Strike one!" cries the umpire.

The second pitch is too low. Once again the batter fails to swing. "Ball one!" the umpire shouts.

Now, here comes the third pitch. Let's see what our batter will do this time. He swings a little too soon. The ball skitters over the ground outside the foul line as it passes third base.

"Foul ball! Strike two!"

(Remember that a foul ball counts as a strike when the batter has fewer than two strikes.)

The count is now one and two. This means one ball and two strikes. In calling the count on a batter, the number of strikes is always given last.

The lead-off man swings mightily at the next pitch.

His bat connects with nothing but thin air.

"Strike three! A strikeout! One out!"

The first batter steps away from home plate and rejoins his teammates on the bench.

The second batter swings at the first pitch made to him. He hits the ball and it soars into the air, to the left side of the diamond. It is too far out to be reached by an infielder. Yet it is not hit deeply enough to be caught by an outfielder. The ball drops safely and the batter reaches first base. Now his aim is to get all the way around the bases and score a run.

"We'll score a million runs! Get in there and sock another hit!" Cries of encouragement to the next batter come from his mates on the bench, or wherever they are waiting.

The batter takes a strike, then a ball, and another ball. A second strike is called by the umpire. Then he calls a third ball. If the pitcher doesn't get the next pitch in the strike zone, the batter will be allowed to go to first base.

The pitch is wide.

"Ball four!" the umpire shouts, and he motions the batter to first base. At the same time the runner on first base moves along to second. Since this is a base on balls no one can tag him out.

Now we have runners on first and second base and only one out. If the next batter makes a good hit, the runner on second base may score a run. With a long hit, for more than a single, both baserunners may score.

This is an exciting point in the game. The catcher walks out to the middle of the diamond to talk to the pitcher. Then one of the infielders hurries over to the mound. They want to be sure that the pitcher is not upset. Encouraging shouts from his other teammates ring in the pitcher's ears.

"Buzz that ball in there, kid!" . . . "Whiz that rock past him!" . . . "Nothing to worry about, you can get 'em out of there!" . . .

Rules do not limit the number of mound conferences, nor specify any time limit. But umpires will come out and break the conference up if too much time is taken.

When their conference is over, the catcher jogs back behind the plate and crouches. He gives the pitcher a signal and holds his mitt up for a target. The signs the pitcher and catcher use have been decided on beforehand by the two of them. Catchers most often signal with one finger against the mitt for a fast ball, and two fingers for a curve.

This time the sign is for a fast ball. The pitch is in the strike zone and the batter hits it sharply. A swift grounder, it skips a little to the shortstop's right. He fields the ball and tosses it to the second baseman, who has run over to the bag.

The second baseman kicks second base before the

**DOUBLE-PLAY**

runner from first arrives, and this man is forced out. Throwing hard and quickly, the second baseman smacks the ball into the first baseman's mitt an instant before the batter's spikes hit the first base bag. Now the batter is out too.

Ballplayers say the infield *got the two*. In other words, two put-outs have been made in one continuous play – for a *double-play*.

Now there are three outs, so the two teams change sides.

In every baseball game, even if both teams are from the same town, one is always considered the *visiting team*. The visiting team opens the game at bat. When it has made three outs, the *home team* comes to bat. In the final inning of a game the home team is at an advantage in having the last chance at bat.

You have probably heard the terms *top of an inning* and *bottom of an inning*. The top of an inning refers to the half of an inning when the visiting team is at bat. The bottom of an inning refers to the half of an inning when the home team is at bat.

For this reason, in keeping score, the top of the scorecard is used for the visiting team. The score of the home team is put at the bottom. Sometimes the bottom of an inning is spoken of as the *last of an inning*.

In our imaginary game we are now at the bottom of the first inning. The lead-off man swings at the very first pitch, hits the ball well. and makes a *line drive* — a hard-hit ball that moves on an even course a few feet above the ground. Unfortunately for him, the ball goes

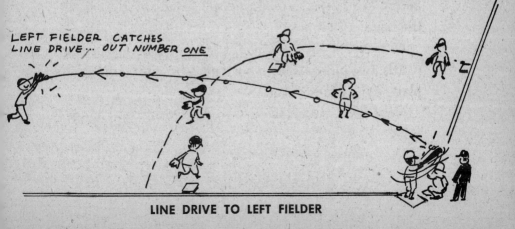

**LINE DRIVE TO LEFT FIELDER**

straight to the left fielder, who catches it, face-high. This is one put-out for the home team.

The next man, who is second in this team's batting order, comes to the plate. He is a left-handed batter. He does not like pitches that curve, and the pitcher knows it. The first pitch is a curve that catches the outside corner of the plate in the strike zone.

The umpire calls, "Strike one!"

The second pitch is a curve that bends too wide to be in the strike zone. It is a ball, the umpire decides.

A third pitch curves over the outer edge of the plate. It is within the strike zone, waist high.

"One ball and two strikes!"

Now the batter crowds closer to the plate. He must swing at any pitch in the strike zone even if it is a curve.

But the pitcher does not throw a curve. He tries to catch the batter off-balance with a pitch just over the inside edge of the plate. The pitch is thrown too far inside. The ball nicks the batter's arm. A batter who is hit by a pitched ball goes to first base, so now there is a baserunner on first.

The third batter is a very fast runner. He is also a fine bunter. A bunt, you remember, is made when a player taps the ball with a loosely held bat instead of swinging at it.

**BUNTING**

When this happens, the ball usually dribbles slowly over the infield ground. To be a fair ball, it must go between the foul lines. A good bunter who is a swift runner can often *beat out a bunt* or get to first base before the throw gets there. Even if he should be thrown out at first base, the runner on first would be advanced to second base. When baserunners advance but the batter is out, the bunt is called a *sacrifice bunt*.

The third batter bunts the first pitch. Slowly the ball dribbles between the mound and first base. The pitcher starts for the ball but the first baseman charges in and grabs it.

The second baseman runs to cover first, and the man

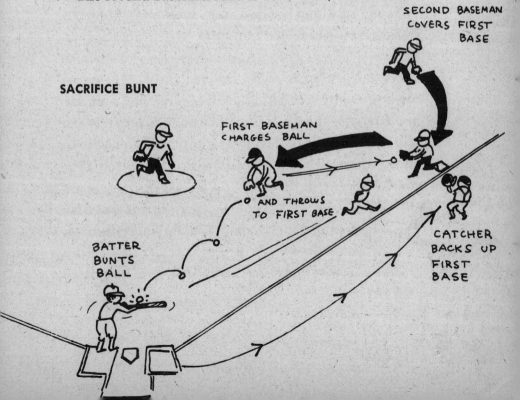

SACRIFICE BUNT

SECOND BASEMAN
COVERS FIRST
BASE

FIRST BASEMAN
CHARGES BALL

AND THROWS
TO FIRST BASE

BATTER
BUNTS
BALL

CATCHER
BACKS UP
FIRST
BASE

on first races to second. But the hurried throw from the first baseman does not reach first until after the bunter has crossed the bag. Now there are baserunners on second and first. There is one out.

The fourth batter swings hard and misses. Then he swings at another pitch and misses. At his third swing, a long high fly ball rises into the sky.

Baserunners may advance only after fly balls are caught. On this play the center fielder is so deep when he catches the fly that the baserunners each *tag up* (stand with one foot touching the base). They advance a base as soon as the ball is caught. Now there are baserunners on second and third with two outs.

A safe hit would probably score both runners, so the pitcher is eager to fool the next batter. He cleverly tricks the batter by throwing with the same motion he has thrown his fast ball, but this time he does not throw it as fast. He "takes something off it," and throws a *change-up* – which means that by releasing the ball with a looser grip, some of the speed is taken away.

The batter's timing is thrown off. He tries to adjust but he can not hit the ball squarely. One long hop and the ball is in the pitcher's glove. He throws to first base for an easy put-out. Three out. Change sides. Fielders come in to bat; batters go out to field.

The inning is over and neither team has scored a run.

# 5. Playing First Base

THE FIRST BASEMAN usually handles the ball more often in a game than any other fielder on the team. He has three main jobs:

1. Field the balls hit into his area that he can reach.
2. Take throws from the pitcher, the catcher, infielders, and outfielders.
3. Work closely with the pitcher and catcher to hold baserunners on first base close to the bag.

A baserunner on first base edges as far toward second as he can. He wants to shorten the distance he will need to run. He may try to *steal*, or run to, second base while a pitch is being made. This is called *stealing* the base because it does not require a hit or a base on balls by the batter to get there.

What makes an ideal first baseman? We asked this question of a man who had played in and managed baseball from Little League teams to the major leagues. This was his answer: "An ideal first baseman is a tall, long-armed guy who throws left-handed. He would have hands as big as hams. They would be as sticky as flypaper when it came to grabbing a baseball. He would be as quick and agile as a monkey. His footwork would be as smooth as a dancing master's. He would be a batter with power to produce the long ball for me."

You can easily see what an advantage it is to be left-handed when you are playing first base. A first baseman's throwing plays are almost always to his right side, to second and third base. They are often split-second plays. A left-handed first baseman can simply draw back his arm and fire the ball. A right-handed

**TAGGING RUNNER SLIDING
BACK TO FIRST BASE**

player would have to pivot for the throw. The time lost could mean the difference between a put-out or the runner's being safe.

However, many first basemen are right-handed throwers. Many are not tall. Even if you are right-handed, if you can catch a ball well and present a good target, you can make yourself into a good first baseman.

To present a good target you have to get near the bag and give the thrower something at which to aim. Your body, your outstretched arms, and your mitt all enter into this. If your teammates have confidence that you will gobble up a poor throw, this also helps your ability to present a good target.

Above all, a first baseman must learn correct footwork. He must be able to step quickly to either side of the bag for wide throws.

When an infielder grabs a batted ball he rarely has time to carefully aim his throw to first base. The first baseman must expect some throws that are wide to one side or the other, high, or in the dirt. A good first baseman practices until he snags them all automatically.

There are three things always to keep in mind:
1. You *must* catch the ball. Stretching, being quick, and moving easily mean nothing if you let the ball go through, under, over, or past you.

**STRETCHING FOR A THROW**

2. You must stretch as far as possible toward the thrower. The split second you save by stretching may get the ball into your mitt just in time to beat the baserunner.

3. You must make contact with the bag when you catch the ball. You can't stand on the bag, always, but you must be in such a position that you can stab it with one foot or the other, before the baserunner touches it.

Some throws will pull you off the bag. You can lunge, dive, or sprawl to tag the runner before he can touch the base. Whether done gracefully or by scrambling, any play you make that gets the baserunner out is a good play.

Suppose your catcher *fields* (picks up) a bunt. The ball is between the foul lines or he has no play. As first baseman, you stand on the side of the bag that is inside

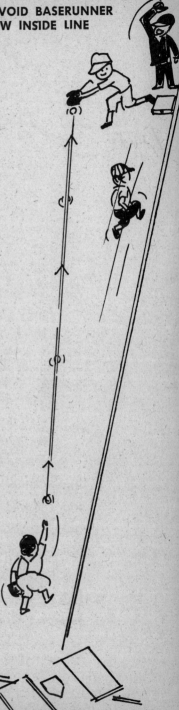

the foul line. The catcher throws well inside the line because there is less risk of hitting the baserunner.

The runner is entitled to three feet as a base path and is no doubt barreling down the line. If the catcher must throw straight down or across the line because his first baseman is out of position, his peg may hit the runner and you will lose a put-out.

Perhaps your catcher drops a third strike. The rules give the batter the right to run on a dropped third strike, if there is no baserunner on first base. The catcher must get the ball to first base ahead of the batter.

Now you step well outside the foul line and hold your mitt out as a target for the catcher. There is less risk of hitting the runner and you can catch the ball without having to lunge in front of the runner charging toward the base.

Watch a first baseman and pitcher when the baseman fields a ground ball and the pitcher covers the bag. Properly executed, this is one of the fine plays in baseball. It takes perfect co-operation

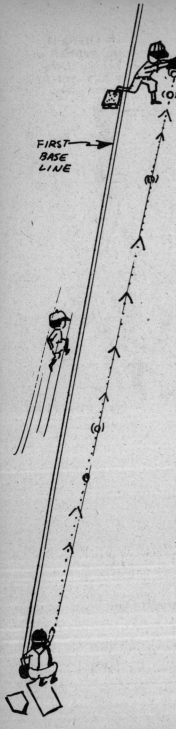

FIRST
BASE
LINE

and timing. Ball and pitcher must get to-gether an instant before the pitcher's foot stabs the bag.

Good timing is seldom accidental. The beautiful timing you see in a game has come from hours of practice by the pitcher and first baseman.

Earlier in the chapter we said that the first baseman holds the baserunner close to the bag. How does he do it? Where should he play? With one foot anchored to the bag? Behind the runner? These are questions the first baseman must answer.

For the most part, he follows a simple rule. If there is no runner on second, he holds the man on first by playing on the bag. When there is a runner on second base, it is less likely that a steal will be tried. (In this case it would be a double-steal with both runners advancing.) The first baseman stays behind the runner where he is in a better position to field the ball, should it be hit his way.

Wherever he plays, the first baseman must always be alert for a quick throw from the pitcher or catcher when there is a runner on first base.

**THROW OUTSIDE LINE TO AVOID BASERUNNER**

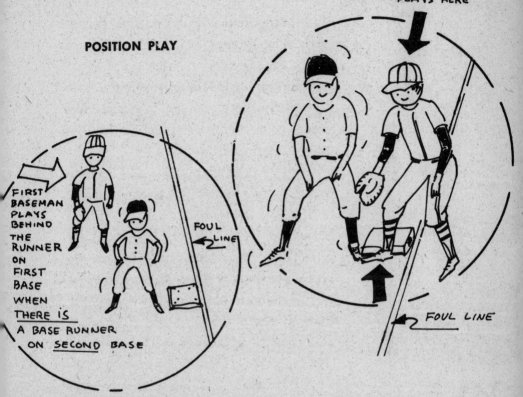

**POSITION PLAY**

IF THERE IS NO RUNNER ON SECOND BASE, FIRST BASEMAN PLAYS HERE

FIRST BASEMAN PLAYS BEHIND THE RUNNER ON FIRST BASE WHEN THERE IS A BASE RUNNER ON SECOND BASE

FOUL LINE

FOUL LINE

### Brief Tips for First Basemen

1. Make a target for the thrower.
2. Know what you will do with the ball if it is hit to you.
3. Be ready to make a throw anywhere after catching the ball. Be alert.
4. Practice an underhand snap throw to use when you field a ball and there is little time to cut down

49

a runner. (A snap of the wrist at the release of the ball, rather than an arm-and-shoulder momentum, supplies the power to the underhand throw.)

5. Study the batters. Play closer to the bag or farther toward second according to where the batter most often hits.

6. Learn to shift your feet to take throws near the bag. Have throws purposely thrown wide to you in practice so that you can perfect your footwork.

**MAKE A TARGET FOR THE THROWER**

# 6. Playing Second Base

THE BALL is handled by the second baseman when it is thrown to him as he covers the bag. If he can field (catch or stop) balls batted into his territory, either on the ground or in the air, he handles those too. His territory is the area from the first baseman's territory to second base. He goes into short right field and across the foul line after short fly balls.

The second baseman is the *pivot man* (the man in the middle) on double-plays started by the third baseman or shortstop.

INFIELDERS

A double-play, you'll remember, means putting two baserunners out in one continuous play. A double-play can pull a pitcher out of trouble when there are men on base and none out or only one out. A double-play can also stop a threatened batting rally. Pitchers have greater confidence when they know that the second baseman and shortstop on their team are expert double-play makers.

The double-play is most often made with a runner on first and the batter hitting a ball on the ground.

Let's say that the shortstop fields a grounder and quickly throws it to second base. The second baseman does not stand on the bag all the time, of course. But he runs swiftly toward the base when he sees where the ball is hit. He catches the ball, stepping on the bag to force out the runner from first. Then he throws the ball as hard and as quickly as he can to the first baseman to beat the batter who is racing for the first-base bag.

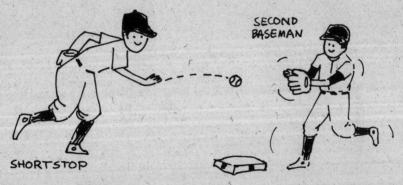

SECOND BASEMAN

SHORTSTOP

**DOUBLE-PLAY — SHORTSTOP TO SECOND BASEMAN**

If the third baseman – or pitcher – fields the batted ball, it is still the second baseman who makes the *force play* at second and hurries a throw off to first. A force play happens when a baserunner must leave his base because the batter, or runner behind him, is entitled to the base he's on. If he doesn't reach the next base before the ball, he becomes a *force out*, the victim of a force play.

Anyone who plays baseball must be able to throw. But the second baseman must be able to throw from any position. He may have to throw while running at top speed. He may be flat on his face after making a diving stop. Sometimes a runner who is coming into second will make it difficult for the second baseman trying to make the double-play. The second baseman may be bowled over, but he has to be able to make the throw while falling or even after being knocked down. Of course, he also has to be able to throw the ball where he wants it to go.

**TO FIRST BASEMAN**

Since the second baseman makes most throws to his left side, you can see that it is an advantage for him to throw right-handed, although there is no rule against a left-handed thrower playing second base.

We have said that baserunners on first sometimes try to steal second. When this happens, the second baseman shares with the shortstop the job of taking the throw from the catcher. Whichever takes the throw tries to tag the runner with the ball before he can touch the base. Ballplayers say that they *put the tag* or *put the ball* on the runner.

Sometimes the catcher's throw will be high or wide. The first duty of the man taking the throw is to catch or block the ball. He must make sure that the baserunner does not get an extra base — run to third — should the throw be bad.

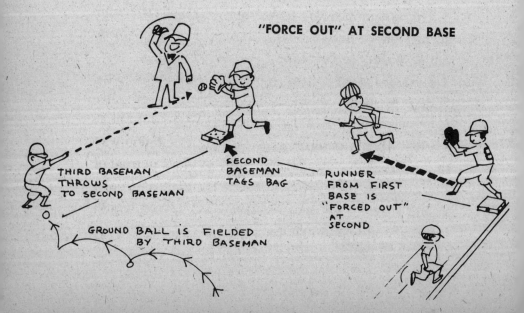

"FORCE OUT" AT SECOND BASE

THIRD BASEMAN THROWS TO SECOND BASEMAN

SECOND BASEMAN TAGS BAG

RUNNER FROM FIRST BASE IS "FORCED OUT" AT SECOND

GROUND BALL IS FIELDED BY THIRD BASEMAN

The second baseman plays toward the first-base side of second base. How far over does he play? It depends on several things.

A smart second baseman studies the batters. Perhaps a certain batter often swings late. Such a batter is likely to hit the ball to the opposite field – ballplayers say the *wrong field*. This means that a right-handed batter, who normally swings and hits most often to left field, might swing late and hit the ball toward right field. The reverse would be true with a left-handed batter.

Some batters pull the ball sharply. This means that they swing a little too quickly and their bat connects with the ball in front of the plate. Their batted balls are likely to go in the direction of the swing. Thus a right-handed pull-hitter knocks the ball toward left field, and a left-handed pull-hitter hits toward right field.

The second baseman remembers whether the batter swings late or pulls the ball. He moves to the right or left according to the batter.

Second baseman and shortstop work closely together. By means of hidden signals they let each other know which man is going to take the throw – if one is made – when a baserunner is on first. A common way of signaling is for the player to hold his glove in front of his face. Only his teammate can see his mouth. An open mouth means, "I'll take the throw." A closed mouth means, "You take the throw."

Sometimes, especially in play below professional level, the shortstop and second baseman plan to take the throw or not according to the way the batter swings. A left-handed batter is more likely to hit toward the first-base side of the infield, so the second baseman stays in position to field a possible grounder while the shortstop covers the bag. A right-handed batter is more likely to hit toward the third-base side of the infield, so the shortstop keeps in position to field a possible grounder and the second baseman covers the bag.

Batters in professional baseball often become skilled at hitting the ball where they want it to go. The second baseman and shortstop try to anticipate — guess, really — which way the batter will try to hit. According to what they decide, one of them stays in position to field the ball. With the pitcher's delivery, the other dashes to

THIRD
BASE

**RIGHT-HANDED PULL HITTER**

the bag, ready to take the throw if one is made.

We have said that on many double-plays the second baseman is the pivot man. He often prefers to catch the ball thrown him as his right foot comes down on the bag. Then he pivots (turns), steps toward first, and cuts loose the throw. A fraction of a second may be saved. It can be the difference between "out" and "safe" at first base. But the second baseman is in position to be upset by the baserunner from first and his throw may be ruined.

Some second basemen choose to stab the bag with the left foot. Then they make the pivot away from the bag toward center field. The throw is made off the left foot.

You must find out which is best for you by experimenting. The idea is to get the throw safely off to first base in time to complete the double-play.

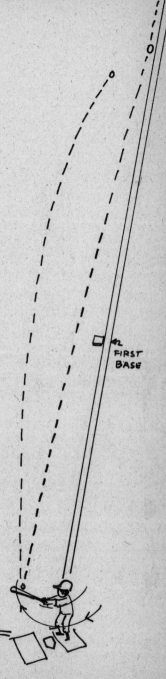

FIRST BASE

**LEFT-HANDED PULL HITTER**

**TELLING WHO WILL COVER THE BAG**

Practice making the double-play again and again and again. What the manager said of first basemen goes for second basemen too. They need the quickness and agility of a monkey, combined with the smooth footwork of a dancing master.

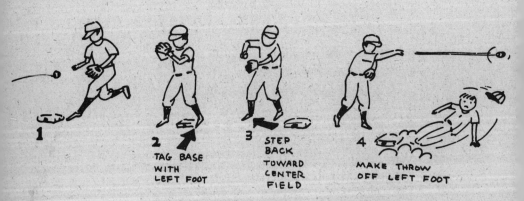

1

2 TAG BASE WITH LEFT FOOT

3 STEP BACK TOWARD CENTER FIELD

4 MAKE THROW OFF LEFT FOOT

**SECOND BASEMAN'S DOUBLE-PLAY PIVOT**

### Brief Tips for Second Basemen

1. Keep your feet behind the bag when tagging.
2. Take enough time in fielding a ground ball to be sure you have it. Except for very slowly hit balls, you never need hurry the throw to first base.
3. Back up second base when the shortstop takes the throw. Back up first base when a catcher drops a third strike.
4. Chase a baserunner caught between bases back toward the bag from which he came. Fake throws and make feints (pretended moves) to confuse him.
5. Go out in the field to help relay the ball when a hit is to deep right field or center field. This means that you will take the throw from the outfielder and speed the play with a throw of your own. Know to which base you should relay the ball.
6. Be ready to take the throw at first base when the first baseman charges in to field a bunt.

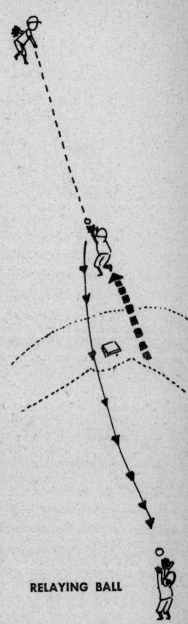

**RELAYING BALL**

# 7. Playing Shortstop

THE BALL comes to the *shortstop* when he takes throws to second base, when batted balls are hit into his territory, and sometimes when he takes throws at third. The shortstop is responsible for the area between second base and the third baseman's territory.

Between the shortstop's territory and that of the third baseman there is a nasty narrow strip. It is very hard to field balls hit there in time to throw the hitter out at first base. Ballplayers refer to this nasty spot as *the hole*.

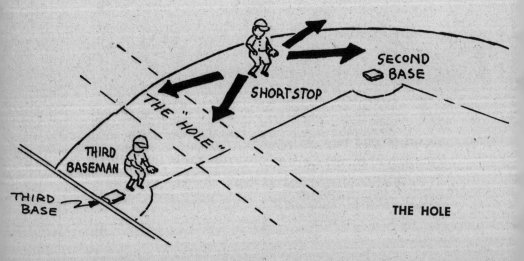

THE HOLE

The shortstop ranges wide to his right to get balls hit into the hole. He races far to his left to grab grounders over – or even to the right of – second base. He sometimes chases fly balls into foul ground beyond the left-field foul line. Normally, a shortstop has more chances of handling the ball than a second baseman. He is expected to protect more territory.

Speed is a great asset in a shortstop. He *must* have quickness and sureness of hand. He needs a stronger arm than the second baseman. Scouts for professional baseball clubs look for two things in a young player – swiftness of foot and a strong arm. The two are perhaps needed more for playing shortstop than for any other position.

If you throw right-handed you are in a better position to play shortstop. A left-handed thrower would be at a great disadvantage.

The shortstop and second baseman must work smoothly together. They need to be equally adept at starting the double-play. As pivot men in the double-play they should both be fast and smooth.

When the shortstop is the middle man in a double-play, his job may be a little simpler. He will be going toward second base to take the throw. It is not necessary for him to make a stop or pivot before he throws.

In a double-play, the shortstop takes the ball thrown to him one stride in front of second base. With his left foot he hits the bag, then he uses the base to push himself off toward the pitcher's mound. As he lands on his right foot, out of the path of a charging baserunner, he throws to first base.

Sometimes the throw from the first baseman or second baseman is on the outfield side of the base path. The shortstop may drag his right foot against the corner of the bag. Then he will step wide toward right field and make his throw to first.

He can also hit the bag with his left foot and step across the sack to throw off his right foot. Some shortstops think this is the best way. Others favor the drag method just described. The drag is probably harder to learn but it does help avoid collision with the baserunner.

Holding runners close to the bag is another duty

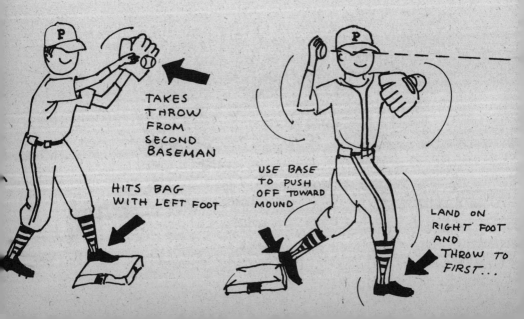

TAKES
THROW
FROM
SECOND
BASEMAN

HITS BAG
WITH LEFT FOOT

USE BASE
TO PUSH
OFF TOWARD
MOUND

LAND ON
RIGHT FOOT
AND
THROW TO
FIRST...

shared by shortstop and second baseman. A pitcher's throw to second — before pitching to the batter — seldom gets the runner out. It may be useful just the same. A runner allowed to take a big lead can sometimes score on a short hit. To keep him close to the bag, the shortstop or second baseman feints dashes toward it. The closer the man is kept to second, the farther he must run when he does go. The extra distance may cause him to be thrown out.

The shortstop is in the best position to direct his team's defensive play. Often a ball is hit into the air where more than one player could make the catch. If it is a ball that the shortstop can reach himself, he shouts so that his teammates know he is going to make the play. Otherwise, he calls out which man is to make the play.

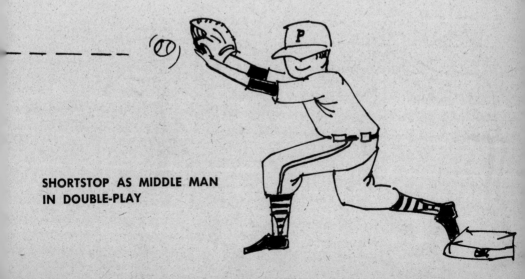

**SHORTSTOP AS MIDDLE MAN IN DOUBLE-PLAY**

The shortstop runs into left field or center field to relay throws from outfielders on deep hits. He acts as relay man for throws to third base, to home plate, or to second base.

The shortstop must take care of second base on plays in which the second baseman goes into the outfield to take a relay throw. The shortstop backs up second base on plays in which the second baseman takes throws to the bag.

All infielders should know the *infield-fly rule*. It is in the *Baseball Rules* book. An infield fly is a fair ball which is hit into the air and can be caught by an infielder with ordinary effort. Say that first and second base, or first, sec-

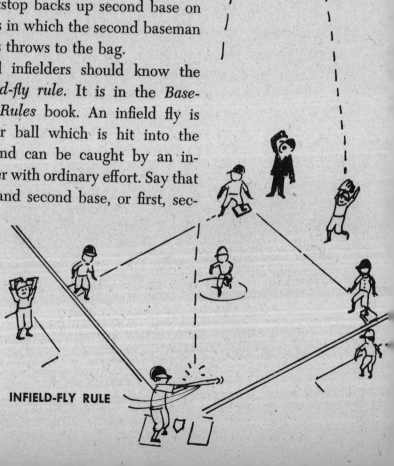

UMPIRE QUICKLY CALLS "INFIELD FLY RULE" BATTER IS AUTOMATICALLY OUT!

**INFIELD-FLY RULE**

SHORTSTOP

SECOND
BASEMAN

**RUNNER CAUGHT "IN A HOT BOX"**

ond, and third base are occupied and there are fewer than two outs. Baserunners are not forced to run when an infield fly is declared.

This is the way the infield-fly rule works. The batter is automatically out the instant the umpire calls the hit ball an infield fly. He calls as quickly as possible. But the ball is not dead. It is still in play. Runners are protected against being forced to run. They may advance at the risk of the ball's being caught. If they do run, they may be put out by a throw to the base that they have left before they can get back and touch it.

Baserunners will rarely be so foolhardy as to try to advance. Should they do so, the shortstop may be in the best position to call to his teammates and tell them where the throw should be made.

Now and then a shortstop will field a grounder and find a runner trapped between second and third base. Usually the runner stands waiting to see what the shortstop will do. Baseball people say that the runner is *in a hot box* or a *rundown*.

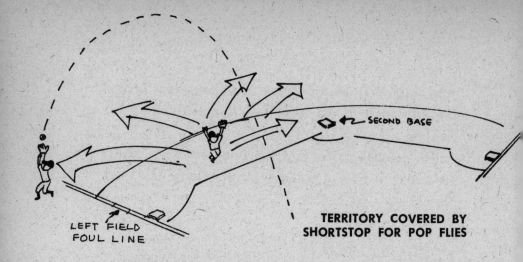

LEFT FIELD
FOUL LINE

SECOND BASE

**TERRITORY COVERED BY
SHORTSTOP FOR POP FLIES**

When this happens, the shortstop should hang onto the ball and charge toward the runner. The runner will have to make a break. It is easy for the shortstop to throw the ball and head him off. The shortstop follows his throw in behind the runner. This keeps him in position for a return throw should the runner reverse and try to get back to second base.

Although a runner sometimes makes it safely to the base, ballplayers think there is no excuse for letting him escape from a hot box.

A man who has worked with young ballplayers for many years summed up the qualities a shortstop needs: "More than any other player, he must be quick. Speed of foot makes him that much better off. He must be able to throw overhand, underhand, or sidearm, hard and fast. He must be a sure catch of pop flies (balls undercut by the batter and popped into the air). He

66

must catch pop-ups anywhere, from the stands behind third, through short left field, to the area behind second base.

"His position makes him best suited to be the team's general in charge of defense. He should be the spark plug of his team. He should be a holler guy who keeps his team fired up."

A baseball team may or may not have a field captain. If it does have one, he is often the shortstop. Whether he is captain or not, the shortstop needs leadership ability.

### Brief Tips for Shortstops

1. Expect every pitched ball to be hit to you. Know what you are going to do with the ball and be sure that you *do* field it.
2. Study the batters. Move right or left according to where the batter most often hits.

**SHORTSTOP RANGES BETWEEN SECOND AND THIRD BASE**

**SHORTSTOP
COVERING
THIRD BASE**

3. Be ready to cover third base when the third baseman handles a bunt.
4. Be ready for throws that pass the pitcher when men are on base.
5. Warn your pitcher not to deliver his pitch until you are back in position after feinting at a baserunner.
6. Before the play, think of what *might* happen and be prepared.

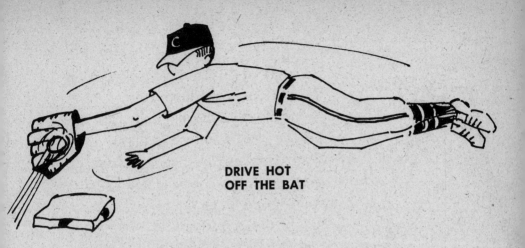

DRIVE HOT
OFF THE BAT

# 8. Playing Third Base

A THIRD BASEMAN handles the ball mainly in two situations. He takes throws to third base. He fields any ball he can reach that is batted into his territory. This is the area from the left-field foul line to whatever distance to his left he can go. In addition, he must field pop fouls between his territory and the stands.

Third base is referred to by ballplayers as *the hot corner* because so many hard-to-handle balls are hit in this area. A right-handed batter who rips the ball down third base way puts the power of his full swing behind it. A ball sliced toward third base by a left-handed batter may slant off the bat very sharply.

When the ball is not a hot drive of this kind, it is likely to be twisting, spinning, squirming, hard to handle, or a bunt that rolls with teasing slowness along the base path. The player guarding the hot corner must be prepared to handle all kinds of difficult plays.

However, the third baseman seldom has as many balls hit his way as the shortstop or second baseman. Right-handed batters do not often pull the ball sharply enough to hit toward third. Left-handed batters are much more likely to hit away from third base. It is usually when they are fooled by a pitch and swing late, or slice an outside pitch, that they hit to third-base territory.

Most balls hit to third base get there so quickly that a third baseman can make almost-errors and still have time to throw the batter out at first base. The third baseman doesn't cover as much territory as the shortstop or second baseman. Therefore he may be slower of foot.

Almost any third baseman would give you an argument if you said the hot corner was easy to play. It is true that at third base a player gets fewer fielding chances than other infielders, but he is expected to add to the team's batting strength. If he is a power hitter who can provide the long ball, he may play the game a long time. This is possible even if he is slow of foot and a weak fielder. However, a third baseman who is also a good infielder is of much more value to his team. A third baseman with poor fielding skills should work hard to improve them.

A third baseman should protect about eighteen feet to his left and twelve feet to his right. The farther he can play from the foul line and still move over to grab balls batted near the line, the smaller the hole between shortstop and third baseman.

The third baseman able to protect the foul line and yet narrow the hole is a big asset to his team. When balls batted down the line get past the third baseman, they usually go for more than one base. Pitchers appreciate a third baseman who can get to such a drive and knock it down so that the batter is held to one base.

One of the most difficult plays a third baseman makes is fielding a *swinging bunt*. A swinging bunt is not really a bunt. It is a pitched ball at which a batter takes a full swing but swings a little too high and causes the overcut ball to trickle over the grass with no more speed than a bunt. It usually has a lot of twisting

LEFT FIELD FOUL LINE  THIRD BASE

**POP-UPS, FAIR OR FOUL**

**FIELDING A SWINGING BUNT**

spin. The third baseman is not expecting a bunt and is playing deep. For this reason he does not get a good jump on the ball.

There is only one way to play a swinging bunt with any hope of throwing out the batter. The player must charge in and grab the ball barehanded. Almost in the same motion as he grabs the ball, he must snap a throw to the first baseman.

"Keep your eye on the ball!" Baseball coaches constantly call out this advice. It is never more necessary than when a third baseman fields a swinging bunt. If he misses his grab for the ball, it may be because he took his eye off the ball and lifted his head too soon.

Third basemen should practice and practice until they are sure they can catch pop flies. A good third baseman gives any pop fly hit into his territory a tough battle. Perhaps a ball that seems headed into the stands or over the fence will be held back by the wind. The baseman looks very foolish if he doesn't go after a pop fly and the ball falls where he could have caught it.

When a baseman smothers those pop-ups, he is helping his pitcher. When you play third base, go over and catch pop flies hit into the pitcher's territory. Remember, he is, first of all, a thrower. As third baseman, you are supposed to be surer of catching a pop fly than the pitcher is.

Today most professional teams play for the big inning — a cluster of runs. Teams swing for the fences and try to knock the ball out of the park. They may not use the sacrifice bunt. Nevertheless a third baseman must be prepared to field bunts coming his way.

With a baserunner on third and less than two out, a third baseman must be on the alert for a possible *squeeze play*. In a squeeze play, there is a signal between the batter and runner as to which pitch the batter will bunt. As the batter bunts the ball, the runner dashes headlong for home plate.

A squeeze play is difficult to break up. The third baseman must grab the ball cleanly and get it to the catcher very fast. Should a squeeze bunt catch him way

THIRD BASEMAN          RUNNER          BATTER

**SQUEEZE PLAY**

**CAUGHT POP FOULS
MAKE PUT-OUTS**

back and unprepared, he has no chance of breaking it up.

At every pitch, a third baseman must be alert and on his toes. If a smart batter sees that the third baseman is asleep, he may bunt toward third even with two outs.

### Brief Tips for Third Basemen

1. Practice catching pop flies wherever you can reach them.
2. Be prepared for a possible bunt, especially when there is danger of a squeeze play.
3. When the batter is left-handed, play toward the plate a little more. A left-handed batter can more easily push a bunt your way.
4. When a runner on third tags up on a fly to the outfield, point at his foot. Until the ball touches the fielder's glove, he cannot dash for home. When he sees you pointing, he will be especially careful to keep contact with the bag. The fraction of a second he loses in getting away may be just enough added time for the throw to nip him at the plate.

**RATTLE THE
BASERUNNER**

# 9. Pitching

THE PITCHER has the ball more often than any other player. His chief role in the game is to pitch the ball in such a way that batters cannot hit it safely far enough and often enough to make more runs than the pitcher's team. Baseball experts say that 75 to 90 per cent of a team's strength is in its pitching. The pitcher has the most exhausting job on a baseball team. He is its first line of defense. With every batter he faces, the pitcher wages a little war.

Control — the ability to throw the ball where he wants it — is a pitcher's most important weapon. But before he can throw anything, a pitcher must care for his arm.

A young pitcher is not taking good care of his arm when he experiments with pitches other than straight pitches. First he must learn how to vary the speed, and how to throw to spots for control. He should wait until his muscles are fully developed before trying curves, screwballs, and sliders.

Experienced pitchers, pitching coaches, and managers all say that a pitcher who can throw his fast ball where he wants it and when he wants it is a better pitcher than one with all kinds of fancy pitches which he can't throw in the strike zone. Practice, *practice*, PRACTICE your control.

Next in importance to control is a good understanding of hitting. A pitcher must study each hitter's way of batting. The more he himself knows about hitting, the better he is able to pitch to the strengths and weaknesses of batters.

Since the catcher is the one who gives the sign for the pitch, the pitcher needs to have confidence in him. At the same time, he must never forget that catchers are human and can make mistakes. If the wrong kind of pitch is made and the batter blasts the ball, it is the pitcher, not the catcher, who is blamed.

The smart pitcher studies the batters constantly. He remembers the type of pitch a batter hits well and the type that gives him trouble. Perhaps the catcher's sign is for a pitch that the batter has hit hard before. The pitcher shakes off the sign — usually by wiggling his glove. Then the catcher will signal for another pitch, or perhaps he will call time and come out to talk to the pitcher. Unless the manager has signaled for a particular pitch, the catcher does not insist on any one pitch. He and the pitcher talk it over. Both of them want a pitch that will fool the batter.

Beginning with his first throw as a pitcher, a boy should try to make his basic pitching motion smooth and natural. There may be a few pitchers with a natural sidearm or underhand delivery. If you have one of these rare natural motions, don't allow anyone to change it. Most young pitchers have a natural three-quarter overhand style. Whatever his style of throw, the pitcher must always remember that the main thing is control over his pitches.

Here is one way to develop control. Find a piece of canvas or any other kind of cloth that is available. Paint lines on it to mark the strike zone. Remember that the strike zone is a rectangle of space the width of home plate (seventeen inches), extending from the top of the batter's knees up to his armpits. Make a frame for your cloth strike zone by nailing four boards

**READY TO PITCH**

together in a rectangle of this size. Fasten the cloth securely to the frame. Then cut holes about three times as big as a baseball in the four corners of it, and anchor the frame firmly in the ground.

Now pitch to it from the pitching distance you are using. If your muscles are still developing, remember that this distance should be less than the regulation sixty feet and six inches.

First aim fifty throws at the high outside hole. Then pitch fifty to the low inside hole. Do the same for the high inside and low outside holes. Keep score of the number of times the ball goes through each hole. Practice in pitching to definite spots is bound to improve your control. Just be careful to limit the time you practice so that you do not risk straining your arm.

Learn to *follow through*. This means to carry your

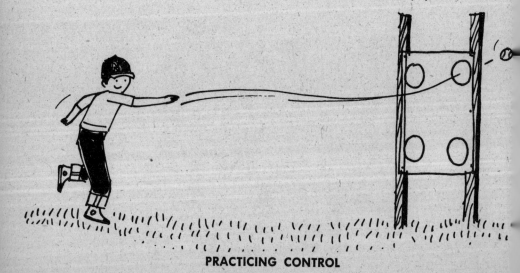

PRACTICING CONTROL

arm through all the way, after releasing the ball. It is important to get the full power of your back and shoulders behind your delivery. Carrying your hand and arm on in a follow-through motion after releasing the ball will help.

The pitcher must have one foot in contact with the pitching rubber when he releases the pitch. You must learn for yourself the part of the slab from which you throw most comfortably. Some pitchers throw from one end of the slab, some from the other end, and some from the center. Other pitchers vary their position with left- or right-handed batters.

A *fast ball* is not the only type of delivery a pitcher needs. A *slow ball* once in a while makes the fast ball seem even faster. Used as a *change-up* – that is a change of pace – a slow ball throws off the batter's tim-

**THE FOLLOW-THROUGH**

ing. Big-league pitchers throw a curve ball to keep the batter from digging in and swinging from the heels on the fast ball. But a curve ball is hard to throw and can strain muscles. Young pitchers shouldn't throw curve balls while they are still growing.

Pitchers are always being asked about their throwing techniques. How do you hold your fast ball? How do you grip your curve? How do you throw a slider? How do you hold your change-up?

Ballplayers refer to the different ways of holding pitches as *fingering*. A fast ball is thrown with the same natural grip you use in picking up a ball you are going to throw. The forefinger and second finger are on top and the thumb is on the bottom. The third and little finger fold naturally against the palm.

The fast ball is delivered straight off the thumb and fingers, without twist to right or left. More or less spin is given the ball by the natural release. A good fast ball will rise as it comes to the plate. Ballplayers say that it is *alive* or that there is *a hop on the ball*.

PITCHER'S GRIP                    FAST BALL

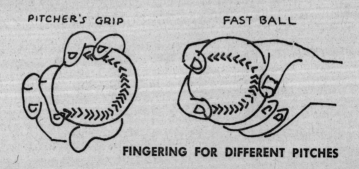

FINGERING FOR DIFFERENT PITCHES

CURVE

A SHARP
SNAP OF
THE WRIST

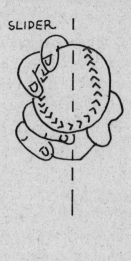

SLIDER

Pitchers work until they can deliver a fast ball, a curve, and a change-up with the same pitching motion. The fingering for each pitch is the same. It is the spin given the ball at release which makes the difference.

A curve is pitched with a sharp snap of the wrist outward or down at the instant of release. The ball rolls off the forefinger. It spins toward the first-base side of the plate when a right-handed pitcher throws it. The left-handed pitcher's curve breaks toward the third-base side of the plate.

Suppose the catcher gives the sign for a change-up pitch. The pitcher grips the ball the same way. He throws it with the same motion. But he lifts the top fingers from the ball as it leaves his hand. A slow curve is pitched with the same wrist snap as the regular curve. But again the top fingers are lifted as the ball is pitched.

You may have heard of a pitch called a *screwball*. It is very hard on a pitcher's arm and is difficult to control. Young pitchers will be well advised not to experiment with a screwball until they are fully grown.

Most pitchers today use a *slider*. It is fingered like a fast ball but delivered with a slight stiff-wrist twist. It comes up to the plate like a curve, then slides or spins.

**ON A WILD PITCH, THE PITCHER RUNS IN TO COVER HOME PLATE**

**BEARING DOWN**

## Brief Tips for Pitchers

1. Practice, practice, practice your control.
2. Make batters hit to get on base. Bases on balls can beat you.
3. Bear down on *all* batters. The "easy-out" hitter too often smashes out a vital hit if carelessly worked on.
4. Stay away from pitches that put extra strain on your arm.
5. Always warm up properly before cutting loose with hard throws.
6. Study the batters. Use your head, your arm, and every weapon you have in the constant battle with them.

7. Practice fielding your position. A pitcher who can field well adds a fifth infielder to his team's defense.

8. Back up third base and home on plays where throws are made to those bases. When there are runners on base, break for the plate if a pitch gets away from you and there is a possibility that the ball may get past the catcher.

MAKING A MITT TARGET

# 10. Catching

THE CATCHER is the workhorse of a baseball team. His role is very important. When his side is in the field he has to be on the alert every second. He must be physically strong and rugged, with a good throwing arm. He needs what players refer to as *baseball savvy*, that is, baseball knowledge.

A clever catcher can bring out the best in the pitcher of a team. It is the catcher's job to make the signs which tell the pitcher the kind of pitches to throw. In order to do this, the catcher must study the batter. How does he stand at the plate? Too close? Then the catcher may signal for curves that break away from him. Does he stand in the front part of the batter's box? Then fast balls may keep him off-balance.

The catcher notes the way opposing batters swing. He keeps track of how well the batter watches pitches. Does the batter keep his eye on the ball all the way and swing only at pitches in the strike zone? Then he is probably a good hitter. Mix up the pitches. Move the ball around. Keep him off-balance. Try not to give him any pitches that are too good.

Does the batter seem overanxious? Is he restless in the box? Give him a slow ball.

Is the batter a guess hitter? Try to give him a pitch that normally would not be thrown in this situation. You have more chance of outguessing him. You may get him to swing at bad pitches.

The catcher makes his mitt a target for his pitcher. He holds the mitt where he wants the pitch. He holds the mitt steady after receiving the ball. This gives the

RIGHT DOWN THE MIDDLE

umpire a chance to judge whether the pitch was in the strike zone.

An umpire calls the pitch as he sees it. If the catcher pulls the ball, it is a kind of insult. The catcher is trying to trick the umpire into calling a ball a strike. Naturally, an umpire doesn't like to be tricked. When a game is played without an umpire, pulling the ball can lead to endless argument.

The catcher squats in a sitting position to give his sign to the pitcher. His feet are fairly close together at this time. The sign – usually the finger system – is given with his bare hand. His knees prevent the catcher's sign from being seen easily by the first- or third-base coach. With his mitt, he shields his bare

**CATCHER SIGNS FOR PITCH HE WANTS**

hand from any batter foolish enough to take his eyes off the pitcher to peek at the catcher's sign.

In the finger system of passing signs, the catcher indicates the pitch he wants by the number of fingers exposed. For example, one finger for a fast ball; two fingers for a curve; three fingers for a change-up; four fingers for a knuckleball or slider or screwball, or whatever other pitch the pitcher uses.

Any time there is a suspicion that a rival player may be stealing the signs, they may be changed and the rival player attempting to read them will cross up his own hitter, if he passes the word as to what pitch is coming.

To receive the pitch, most catchers take a stance that straddles the plate. That means the feet are eighteen to twenty-one inches apart. Normally the toes will turn out slightly. The main thing is to assume a stance that will be comfortable.

There is no set rule for the signs that catchers use. If there is any reason to think that rival players are getting them, the signs may be changed from game to game. They may be changed *during* a game, for that matter.

The catcher may brush his right hand across his right shoulder if he wants the pitch high and outside. He may brush or touch his left shoulder with his mitt for a high pitch inside. Touching the right or left shin

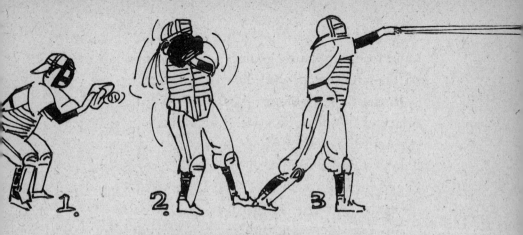

**PEG TO SECOND BASE**

guard can be a sign for a pitch low and inside or low and outside, according to which shin is touched.

A catcher should have a strong arm. He must be prepared for attempts to steal bases. Whenever there is a baserunner, there is risk of a base-stealing attempt.

In receiving the pitch, the catcher usually steps forward with his left foot. His *pegs* – throws to a base to cut down a baserunner – are made off the right foot. He cocks his arm and snaps the throw from approximately his right ear.

Few baserunners will ever be thrown out by the catcher who uses vital time in taking his arm all the way back to throw. The catcher who takes an extra stride before whipping his peg will not throw many runners out either.

A catcher always wears a mask to protect his face. But the bars of a catcher's mask interfere with his vision when he is locating a pop fly, so he yanks off the mask. Now what can he do with it?

He either carries the mask with him until he is under the pop, or he flings the mask as far away as he can. A catcher who stumbles over his own mask when chasing a foul pop feels rather foolish. If his team loses a put-out, he will feel even worse.

Experienced catchers turn after foul pops according to the direction of the pitch. Pops fouled from pitches coming to the plate on the glove side will be to the left. Pitches to the bare-hand side will be fouled to the right. After he takes his turn, the catcher throws his head back to locate the ball. If possible, he gets right under the ball as it is coming down. Then he backs up a little in order to catch the ball in front.

Another important part of a catcher's job is to defend the plate when a baserunner tries to score. This does not mean simply to straddle the plate and wait. Without the ball, you can't possibly put the tag on a runner. Get the ball first. Then block the plate or dive for the runner.

Young catchers should practice their footwork. Smooth footwork is as important to a catcher as it is

**MAKE SURE YOU
HAVE THE BALL**

**BLOCK LOW
PITCHES ON THE KNEES**

to a first baseman. The catcher must shift his feet to meet the pitch. A good system of shifting the feet is to make the first step with the foot farthest from the pitch.

Suppose the pitch is wide to the right. Shift the left foot behind the right. Then take a wide step with the right foot.

Suppose the pitch is wide to the left? Shift the right foot behind the left and take a wide stride with the left.

Sometimes pitches are into the dirt. Experienced catchers handle these low pitches by dropping to their knees. Use your body to block the ball if you must. A ball that gets away from the catcher may cost his team a ballgame.

MAKE A BASKET OF MITT AND HAND TO CATCH POP FOULS

### Brief Tips for Catchers

1. Make a target with your mitt for your pitcher, and hold it steady.
2. Practice judging and catching pop fouls.
3. Practice getting your mask off when a pop foul is hit. Throw it clear of your path right away or carry it until you locate the ball. In either case there will be less danger of stepping on it.
4. Practice your footwork until you can shift your feet smoothly and automatically on wide pitches.
5. Practice handling bunts near the plate.
6. Study the other team's batters. This is a practice that must go on and on.

IF YOU EXPECT A BUNT,
DON'T CROUCH WAY DOWN..
HOLD YOUR MITT A LITTLE
HIGHER AND MOVE YOUR
RIGHT FOOT BACK SO YOU
ARE READY FOR A "QUICK
JUMP" ON THE BUNTED BALL

**HANDLING BUNTS AND POP FOULS**

# 11. Playing the Outfield

IN GENERAL, an outfielder handles the
ball only when it is batted into his territory. He may also be called on at times
to take a wild throw that gets past an
infielder.

There is an old baseball joke that says
an outfielder ought to pay to get into
the park. It means, of course, that outfielders have very little to do in the field.
You would have a hard job finding an
outfielder who would agree.

It is true that an outfielder averages
only about three chances per game to
field the ball. Nevertheless, he must be
as alert and on his toes as any other
member of the team. An outfielder *covers*
(patrols) a much larger territory than an
infielder. What is more, if he *muffs*

(misses) a ball hit into his area, there is no hope of recovering it in time to get the batter out.

Outfielders need patience. If you are tense, nervous, or impatient, you should not try to play the outfield. Outfielders must expect to wait and wait and wait. Yet they must constantly be on the alert. When the ball finally comes their way, they must be eager to play it.

At every pitch an outfielder rises onto his toes. He has to expect that every pitched ball may be hit to him. He must always plan what he will do with the ball if it is hit to his field.

Outfielders and relief pitchers who warm up in the bullpen all through a game have something in common. Although the relief pitcher may never be called to the mound, he may throw enough to pitch an entire game. The outfielder may not have a ball batted his way once all through the game. Yet he comes up on his toes and tenses his muscles, ready to start, again and again. During any game, he uses almost enough energy to have fielded every single ball.

Left field, center field, and right field are not all played the same way. Right fielders protect the right foul-line area. They must play reasonably close to the line. Left fielders protect the left foul-line area, and they too must play fairly close to the line. This leaves the center fielder with more ground to cover than either of his teammates. The center fielder needs to be quick and fast of foot.

Outfielders should practice fielding ground balls as well as catching fly balls and line drives. They must be sure that ground balls do not go past them. A ball that gets past an outfielder almost always allows the batter to stretch his hit for an extra base. The other base-runners advance farther than they could have if the ball had not gotten past the outfielder.

Outfielders back up throws made to first, second, and third base. Right fielders back up first base. Center fielders back up second base. Left fielders back up third base.

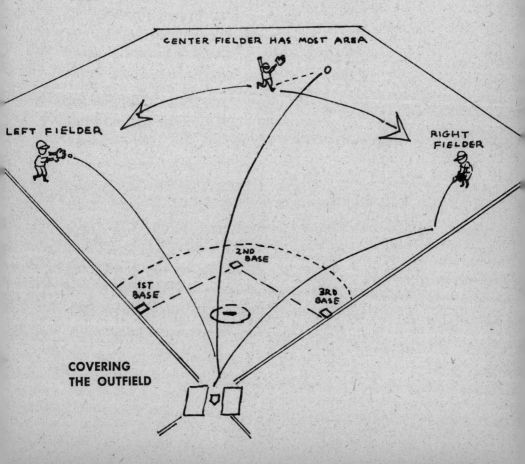

CENTER FIELDER HAS MOST AREA

LEFT FIELDER

RIGHT FIELDER

2ND BASE

1ST BASE

3RD BASE

COVERING THE OUTFIELD

One of the greatest fielding outfielders of all time was the late Tris Speaker. He is enshrined in the Baseball Hall of Fame. Here is what he said to young ballplayers about outfielding:

"Getting the jump on the ball is the most important thing about outfielding. Getting the jump means making a quick start when the ball rides off the bat."

Only with practice can you learn to judge a hit ball by listening to the crack of the bat. You must be able to go back fast for long hits. You must know how to come in fast for short fly balls. Study the batters and the pitches — whether outside, inside, high or low. Pay attention to the wind and the situation of the game. Learn to play with all these things in mind.

When you catch the ball, try to be in position to get off a throw as soon as the catch is made. You must decide for yourself whether to attempt a diving catch. Unless the winning run or tying run is going to score on a hit, it is probably better to play safe and let the ball fall in front where you can be pretty sure of getting it. A successful, diving, circus catch is a great thing

1. DIVING CATCH  2. ROLL OVER  3. BACK ON YOUR FEET  4. GET THAT BALL OFF TO THE INFIELD

**DON'T TRY SPECTACULAR CATCH, UNLESS NECESSARY**

to bring off, but if the dive fails, the ball is almost sure to get past you, and the game may be lost.

An outfielder who catches a ball hit into the air must know where he is going to throw it. The same thing holds true if he fields a grounder or a fly that he could not reach before the ball hit the ground. When there are baserunners, the outfielder must get rid of the ball as quickly as possible in order to keep the runners from advancing.

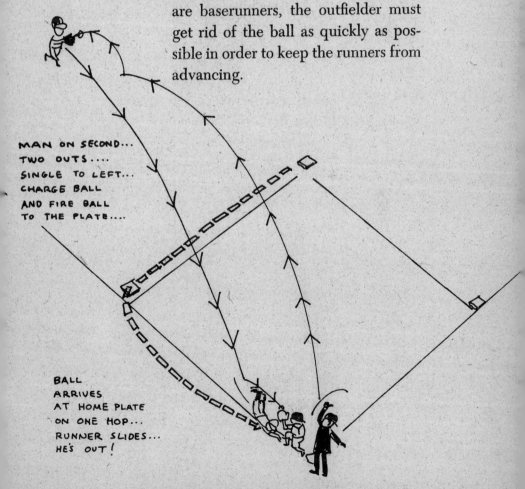

MAN ON SECOND...
TWO OUTS....
SINGLE TO LEFT...
CHARGE BALL
AND FIRE BALL
TO THE PLATE....

BALL
ARRIVES
AT HOME PLATE
ON ONE HOP...
RUNNER SLIDES...
HE'S OUT!

**OUTFIELDER'S HUSTLE GETS AN OUT**

If an outfielder goes after a fly ball that could also be caught by another fielder, he is expected to shout, "I'll take it!" If he feels that another fielder has a better chance of catching the ball, the outfielder yells, "You take it!"

Ground balls *must not* get through an outfielder. If necessary, he should throw his body on the ball to keep it from going past him.

We have said that an outfielder must keep alert and be eager to field balls hit his way. He must not be too eager, however. It is a good practice to count one before starting for a line drive. It is far better to allow the hitter a single than to start too quickly, misjudge the drive, and let him stretch the hit to two or three bases or perhaps a home run.

IT IS BETTER TO PLAY LINER ON FIRST BOUNCE AND HOLD BATTER TO A SINGLE..

PLAYING SAFE CAN BE THE SMART PLAY

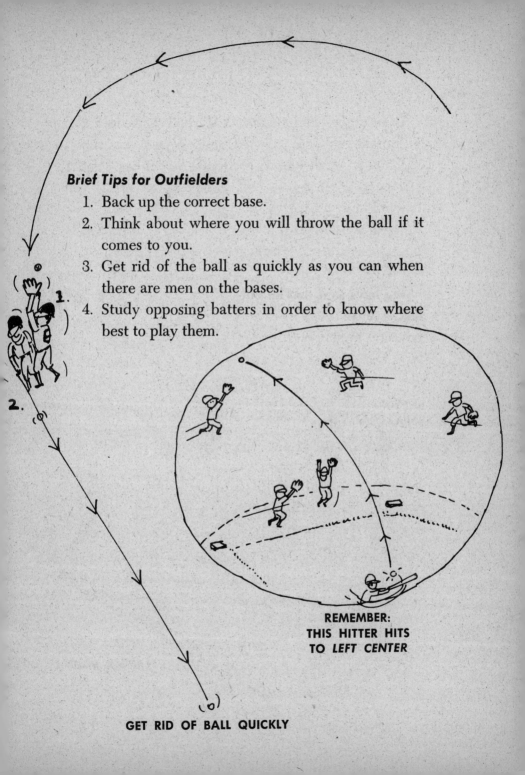

### Brief Tips for Outfielders

1. Back up the correct base.
2. Think about where you will throw the ball if it comes to you.
3. Get rid of the ball as quickly as you can when there are men on the bases.
4. Study opposing batters in order to know where best to play them.

**REMEMBER:**
**THIS HITTER HITS**
**TO *LEFT CENTER***

**GET RID OF BALL QUICKLY**

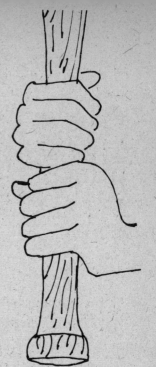

**CHOKING GRIP**

# 12. Hitting and Base-Running

Every member of a baseball team has his place in the batting order. When his turn comes up, he goes to bat. For this reason, hitting is a concern of every ballplayer.

A good hitter must win his share of the battles with the pitcher. No batter consistently hits safely five or more times out of ten times at bat. But to be a good hitter a batter must hit the ball solidly more times than not.

Ballplayers say that they *got good wood on the ball* or that they *hit the ball with the fat part of the bat*, meaning that they connected solidly with the ball. Still, a batter may hit the ball solidly on good wood only to have one of the seven fielders behind the pitcher get in front of the drive and take the hit away from him.

3 HITS | IN 10 AT BAT = .300

**FINE HITTING**

In figuring batting averages, perfect is equal to 1.000. If you batted ten times and made ten safe hits, you would bat 1.000. You would also have every team in baseball anxious to get you.

Suppose you batted ten times and made three hits. To find your batting average, divide three (the number of hits) by ten (the number of times at bat) and carry the division to three decimal places. Your average would be .300. With .300 or more, you are a very good hitter.

### Hitting

A good hitter has to have sharp eyes and quick, sure reflexes. His timing must be nearly perfect. He needs strength of shoulders, arms, and wrists. These are physical attributes that can be sharpened and increased by practice, but nature must provide them in the first place. That is why many baseball people say that good hitters are born, not made.

101

The good hitter must develop judgment and self-confidence. These are qualities which can come through experience. For example, with experience, you will be able to decide about the type and size of bat that fits you best.

Your swing should be smooth and level, with the bat cutting through the air parallel to the ground. A batter who *chops* wood – swings his bat as he would an ax, with a downward trend – beats the ball into the dirt. His batted balls are likely to be fielded, causing him to be thrown out at first base. The batter who swings with

READY FOR THE PITCH

KNEE IS FIRMLY SET

STEP FORWARD

MEETING THE BALL

an upward trend undercuts the ball. He is most likely to hit easy fly balls or pop-ups that are *camped under* (waiting to be caught) by a fielder for put-outs.

Suppose you are up at the plate. As the pitcher begins his delivery motion, you grip your bat. You bring it forward smoothly and on a level. Into the swing goes the strength of shoulders, arms, and wrists. As you cock your wrists, step toward the pitcher with the forward foot. Keep the leg almost straight, with the knee firmly set. You will be hitting off your front leg, with the axis of your weight over the rear leg.

Do not hurry your swing. Only when bat and ball meet should you uncock your wrists. Through wrist snap that adds speed at the moment of contact, you pour power into your swing.

The good hitter keeps his eye on the ball from the moment it leaves the pitcher's hand. There is only a fraction of a second in which to decide whether to swing. He watches the ball as long

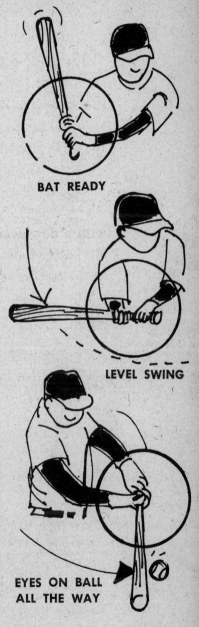

BAT READY

LEVEL SWING

EYES ON BALL
ALL THE WAY

**OVERSTRIDER**

as possible. Before he swings at it, he wants to be sure that the pitch is in the strike zone. He knows that the umpire will call the pitch a ball if it is not in the strike zone. Four balls and he will have a *walk* — a base on balls. The batter knows that a base on balls often unsettles a pitcher even more than a hit.

The stride is an important part of the swing. A young batter should experiment until he finds the stride that is exactly right for him. Do not overstride. The overstrider cannot pivot for his follow-through. He is off-

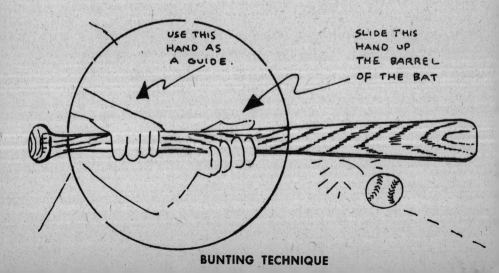

USE THIS HAND AS A GUIDE.

SLIDE THIS HAND UP THE BARREL OF THE BAT

**BUNTING TECHNIQUE**

balance and wastes most of his power. The pitcher is apt to pitch him curves and he will not be in position to step into the ball.

One batting skill that can be – and should be – developed through practice is the bunt. There are times when strategy demands that even a .300 hitter should bunt. The batter shifts his grip on the bat when bunting. He holds the bat loosely and lowers it, parallel to the ground, as the pitcher delivers. He slides his upper hand up the barrel of the bat. His lower hand is used as a guide to get the bat in front of the pitch. The secret of a good bunt is to make the impact of ball and bat as soft as possible.

Of course, the batter knows when he is going to bunt a pitch, but he must keep this secret from the opposing team. Not until *after* the pitcher delivers, does he drop his bat to bunting position.

Getting his safe hits when he is up at the plate is most satisfying to a ballplayer. A good day at the plate erases any memory of *bobbles* (mistakes) in the field. The hitter who has gone *three-for-four* or *four-for-four* (made three or four safe hits in four times at bat) feels that everything is right with the world. On the other hand, if the pitcher hasn't allowed him a hit and he has had a bad day at the plate, he feels quite miserable. It may be a good idea to keep away from him for the time being.

### Base-Running

Even the poorest of batters will sometimes get on base and become a baserunner. For this reason, all ball-players are concerned with base-running. When he has reached first base without being put out, the batter becomes a baserunner. Then he has an opportunity to help his team. Good base-running adds to a team effort and contributes greatly to team hustle and aggressiveness. The hustling, aggressive team wins games.

Knowing when to run is important to good base-running. This calls for a sharp eye and a good head. Effective base-running is much more than just stealing bases.

"If you have fast men on your club," a big-league manager once said, "use them. Develop the habit in your men of rounding the base on every hit. Have them ready to take that extra base at the slightest opportunity. The other team soon looks for your club to pull a daring play. They get overanxious. The fielders hurry throws. They try to grab ground balls too quickly and miss the 'handle' on the ball. Soon your men are getting that extra base handed to them on a silver platter."

The good baserunner is constantly alert. He knows at all times how many men are out. He keeps an eye on the coaches at first and third base. He depends on them and obeys their signs. He always watches the runner ahead of him. Nothing makes a baserunner look more foolish than to have him wind up on the same base with another runner.

### Base-Stealing

Quite often the aim in modern baseball is to play for the big inning — the cluster of runs. Stealing bases, or any risky play which might break up what promises to be a big inning, has no place in a good manager's strategy. Yet there are times when a stolen base adds so much that the risk is taken.

It is rarely a good idea to attempt a steal with nobody out. A steal is tried only when there is a chance of an important run, or when a member of the defensive team is not alert.

Sliding head first into a base is not recommended. There is too much risk of injury. Instead, ballplayers should learn to slide feet first. They use two different methods. One way is to slide into the bag on the right leg and

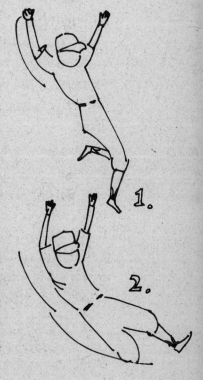

1.

2.

3.

**GOOD BASERUNNERS KNOW HOW TO SLIDE**

hook the sack with the left toe. In the other method, the player slides to the side away from the man covering the bag and gives him as small a tag target as possible.

Learn to relax and lose any fear you may have about sliding. Practice until it becomes automatic. Wear sliding pads if possible. Once you have started a slide never change your mind. The half slide is a good way to get hurt.

A slide serves two purposes: (1) It avoids a tag by the baseman. (2) It prevents overrunning the base and being tagged out after the throw has been beaten.

The smartest baserunner will sometimes find himself trapped. If this happens to you, don't give up without a battle. Keep the rundown going. A fielder may become overanxious and mishandle the ball. Even though you are eventually out, by jockeying back and forth you give baserunners behind you a chance to advance to the farthest base possible.

**KEEP THE RUNDOWN GOING**

# 13. Strategy — Offensive and Defensive

THERE ARE many strategic moves made in baseball games that help teams win. The manager determines strategy for a professional club. For a boys' team, strategy is decided by the coach. In both cases, signs from the bench (given by the coach or manager) are relayed to batters and baserunners by one of the base coaches.

## Coaching

All teams use a coach at first base and one at third base. Besides relaying signs, these coaches help baserunners by keeping track of the ball. They warn runners when to scurry back to a base from which they are leading off when a play on them is about to be made.

Big-league teams have men who are specialists in coaching, but not all clubs can afford extra coaches. Players who are not likely to come to bat during the inning — or substitute players not in the line-up — serve as coaches.

One big-league manager who was asked what qualities were needed by a coach replied, "Be smart, sensible,
and sharp as a tack. Be a good listener and ready with
sound advice. Be able to make decisions right away, and
willing to accept the blame if the decision is wrong. Be
ready to take advantage of any opening you see. Be
willing to accept without protest blame for errors that
may not have been yours. Be prepared to get no credit
when things turn out right. Own the coolness and ability to direct traffic at the busiest corner of your city.
Have all these qualities and you can *try* to be a coach!"

### Defensive Strategy

Defensive strategy is fairly cut and dried. The team
practices the following defensive plays: (1) *Pick-off
plays* — the timing between pitcher and infielder, who
is going to attempt to get to a base before the runner
leading off can get back, take the pitcher's throw, and
tag him out. (2) *Cut-off plays* – cutting off throws from
the outfield when it is apparent that the throw is too
late, and either making a play for a baserunner attempting to take a base, or scaring him back from attempting
to advance the extra base. (3) Throwing to the proper
base. (4) Defense against the sacrifice bunt, that is,
making sure who is going to cover what base so that
the bunt won't turn into a hit, and defense against the
squeeze play. (5) Pulling the infielders in on the grass

to cut off a possible run at the plate if a ground ball is hit and fielded. (6) Playing the infield deep and trying to get the double-play.

There is no secrecy about defensive strategy and the manager or coach shouts directions as to the pattern to use.

## Offensive Strategy

It is the offensive strategy that the base coaches direct. They do this by flashing signs to batters and baserunners. The sign may tell the player to *hit* or *take* a pitch, to steal or to play it safe. Although coaches may use various sets of signs, they are always kept as simple as possible.

The *take* sign tells the batter not to swing at the upcoming pitch. For this sign, the coach might touch flesh after touching cloth. He might touch cloth after touching flesh, or he might touch flesh after touching flesh. Sometimes the take sign is made by one hand or the other touching the letters or club insignia on the shirt front. Coaches have many different ways of flashing this signal to the players.

The *hit* sign which gives the batter the manager's approval to swing at the upcoming pitch may be any of these signs or something altogether different.

Next time you watch a ballgame, keep your eye on the base coaches. One of them – or both – will make dozens of different motions. If you didn't know that the motions were made for a purpose, you might think the coach had a nervous ailment that made him jumpy. Only a few of the many motions carry a message (give a sign). The other motions are meaningless. Opponents are constantly watching. If they can discover the signs the other team uses, you can see what a big advantage this gives them. By making many, many motions, the coaches hope to confuse their opponents.

For baserunners, however, coaches do use certain visible signs. Swinging a hand inward toward the chest tells the runner to keep coming. Pushing the hands away from the body with palms outward orders the runner to stop, to hold back. Lifting the arms above the head means that there is no need to slide. Holding the hands parallel to the ground with palms down is the sign for the runner to slide or "hit the dirt."

It is the third-base coach's responsibility to send a runner home or hold him at third. It is the coach who decides whether a fly ball is hit deeply enough for the runner to risk *tagging up* – keeping one foot in contact with the base – and dashing for the plate after the catch. If he decides to send the runner home, the coach stands as close to the runner as the boundary of the coaching box allows.

The runner tags up. He pays no attention to the third baseman, who is probably pointing at his foot.

He pays no attention to the ball out in the field. A bare instant before the ball contacts the fielder's glove, the coach yells, "Go!" He is not trying to cheat. He knows that the runner cannot legally take off before the ball strikes the fielder's glove. But the coach yells the starting signal because he knows that by the time the runner's reflexes are set in motion, the ball will have hit the fielder's glove.

After reading this book, a veteran big-league player told the author that "any manager could add a lot more to the strategy outlined here and not cover everything. Additions to old strategy, new quirks, or even entirely new strategy come often."

## 14. Keeping Score

SCOREKEEPERS MAY DIFFER a little in the way they keep score, but there are certain things that they all do. They all number positions in the field the same way.

Pitcher is Number 1. Catcher is Number 2. First base is Number 3. Second base is Number 4. Third base is Number 5. Shortstop is Number 6. Starting in left field, the outfield positions are numbered 7, 8, and 9.

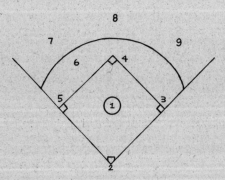

STANDARD NUMBERING FOR POSITIONS

A score card has squares for each inning for each player in the batting order. This is the way a score card looks before being used.

| PLAYER | 1 | 2 | 3 | 4 | 5 | 6 | 7 | 8 | 9 |
|--------|---|---|---|---|---|---|---|---|---|
|        |   |   |   |   |   |   |   |   |   |
|        |   |   |   |   |   |   |   |   |   |
|        |   |   |   |   |   |   |   |   |   |
|        |   |   |   |   |   |   |   |   |   |
|        |   |   |   |   |   |   |   |   |   |
|        |   |   |   |   |   |   |   |   |   |
|        |   |   |   |   |   |   |   |   |   |
|        |   |   |   |   |   |   |   |   |   |
|        |   |   |   |   |   |   |   |   |   |

**SCORECARD**

Let's score the inning that our imaginary teams played back in Chapter 4.

White, the lead-off man in the top of the first inning, struck out. Practically all scorers show a strikeout with a K. So we will show that White struck out by putting a K in the square opposite his name.

Tomson was the second batter. His little blooper fly to left field fell safely. To show that he reached first base, we make a line straight up and down in the right side of his square. Above this vertical line we make a

| PLAYER | | 1 |
|---|---|---|
| White 8 | | K |
| Tomson 4 | | ˥ |
| Loomis 6 | | 6-4 ʷ |
| Jones 9 | | 4-3 |
| Verdi 7 | | |
| Grabbe 3 | | |
| Karn 5 | | |
| Stopper 2 | | |
| Thrower 1 | | |
| | | ¹⁄₀ |

separate, shorter line slanting upward toward the left. This shows that he reached first base on a hit which went to the left side of the diamond. We also add a horizontal line to the vertical line in Tomson's square because he reached second base – half way to completing his square–when the third batter was given a base on balls.

Loomis was the name of the third batter in the top of the inning. Loomis received a base on balls. Some scorers make two small B's in the upper right-hand corner to stand for *base on balls*. Our system is to use a vertical line to show that Loomis reached first base and then to place a small W (walk) at the upper right.

Do you remember what Jones, the fourth batter, did? He hit a sharp ground ball that skipped a little to the shortstop's right. The ball was fielded cleanly and the shortstop tossed to the second baseman. Loomis was forced out. The second baseman threw hard and quickly to first base. The ball arrived before Jones could touch the bag and Jones was out, too.

This action is shown on the score-card by making a 6-4 in Loomis' square. This shows that shortstop, Number 6, threw to second baseman, Number 4, for the put-out. In the square opposite Jones we write 4-3. This indicates that second baseman, Number 4, threw to first baseman, Number 3, to retire Jones.

The home team in our make-believe game had its shortstop, Smith, leading off. Smith hit a pitch solidly on the good wood of his bat. But, remember, it went on a line straight at the left fielder. We show the action in Smith's square by L-7, lined out to left field.

The second batter in the bottom of the inning was Johnson, right fielder, who bats left-handed. The pitcher threw him curves until the count was one and two. Then a fast ball pitched too far inside hit the batter on the arm.

We make a vertical mark in Johnson's square. Then to indicate how he reached base, we make a small HB (hit batsman) at the upper right.

**BOTTOM OF SCORECARD**

| PLAYER | | 1 |
|---|---|---|
| Smith | 6 | L-7 |
| Johnson | 9 | HB |
| Speed | 8 | |
| Parks | 5 | F-8 |
| Modjewski | 3 | 1-3 |
| Maxon | 7 | |
| Down | 4 | |
| Receivo | 2 | |
| Hurler | 1 | |
| | | 0 |

117

Our third batter was the center fielder, Speed. He is very fast and an excellent bunter. His bunt was so good that neither the first baseman nor the pitcher could field the ball in time to throw him out. It was a hit. We add a horizontal mark to the vertical line in Johnson's square to show that he moved to second base. We make a vertical line in the right portion of Speed's square to show that he reached first base. We make a small, separate, slanting line in the upper right corner to show that the hit went to the right side of the diamond.

The fourth batter was Parks, a third baseman who often hits a long ball. This time his long ball was caught by the center fielder for the second out. It is shown by F-8. We add a vertical mark to the horizontal and vertical lines in Johnson's square to show that he moved to third base after the catch. We add a horizontal mark to the vertical line in Speed's square to show that he moved to second base.

Next, Modjewski, the tall and husky first baseman, came to the plate. Modjewski swung mightily but topped a one-hopper to the pitcher and was thrown out at first to retire the side. Modjewski's out is shown on the scorecard as 1-3, which indicates that Number 1, the pitcher, fielded a grounder and threw to Number 3, the first baseman, who made the put-out.

If one of the batters had hit for more than a single,

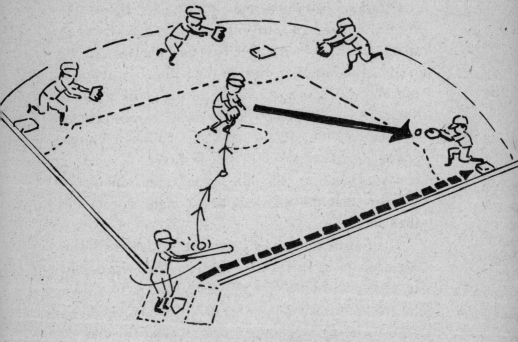

**ONE HOPPER TO PITCHER
WHO THROWS RUNNER OUT**

small separate lines would have been made in the upper right corner of his scorecard box – two lines for a double, three for a triple, four for a home run. The lines would have been slanted to show the direction of his hit, and his progress around the bases would have been shown by horizontal and vertical lines to complete the square. An X within this square will indicate that he had scored a run.

**CATCHER AND UMPIRE DO NOT ALWAYS AGREE**

### Umpires

Umpires are important in a baseball game. They do not wear a uniform as the players do but they usually dress alike in dark trousers and coats, or dark shirts.

The umpire-in-chief stands behind the catcher. He rules on whether pitches are strikes or balls. If the ball crosses any part of the plate in the strike zone, the umpire calls it a strike. If the pitch is wide, too close to the batter, higher or lower than the strike zone, the umpire calls it a ball.

STRIKES

BALLS

**THREE-AND-ONE COUNT
ON BATTER**

Umpires use the right hand to signal strikes and the left hand to signal balls. There is no set rule as to what motion shall be made. Some umpires merely point a finger toward the ground. Others are more dramatic, especially in the case of a third strike, when they may put their whole body into the act.

SAFE

OUT

**BASE UMPIRE SIGNS**

Base umpires signal that a runner is safe by spreading or swinging their hands in a plane parallel to the ground. A put-out of a baserunner is indicated by jerking the right thumb over the shoulder. Again, there is no set rule. Some umpires use a push-pull gesture of the right fist to make the *out* sign.

121

Many books bigger than this one have been written about position play, hitting, base-running, and all the other aspects of baseball. Even then, *everything* about baseball has never been included in one book. Learning about baseball is a process that can go on and on and on.

No matter what you read, playing the game itself is still the best way to learn to play better baseball. So, here's hoping that you are out there when the umpire shouts, "Batter up!"

**Index**

# Index

(Page references indicate both text and illustration.)